The STOP Domestic Violence Program

THIRD EDITION, REVISED AND UPDATED

Also by David B. Wexler

The Adolescent Self
The PRISM Workbook
The Advanced PRISM Workbook
Domestic Violence 2000

A Norton Professional Book

The STOP Domestic Violence Program

THIRD EDITION, REVISED AND UPDATED

Innovative Skills, Techniques, Options, and Plans for Better Relationships

GROUP LEADER'S MANUAL

David B. Wexler, Ph.D.

W. W NORTON & COMPANY
New York · London

All material in this book is protected by copyright. To reproduce or adapt it, in whole or in part, for any purpose whatsoever, by any means, including photocopying, reprinting, or any form of computer storage or programming, is not only a violation of copyright law, but is unethical and unprofessional. Thank you for your cooperation in complying with these standards.

Copyright © 2013, 2006, 2000 by David B. Wexler

Previous editions published under the titles DOMESTIC VIOLENCE 2000 and
STOP DOMESTIC VIOLENCE

All rights reserved
Printed in the United States of America

For information about permission to reproduce selections from this book, write to
Permissions, W. W. Norton & Company, Inc., 500 Fifth Avenue, New York, NY 10110

For information about special discounts for bulk purchases, please contact W. W. Norton
Special Sales at specialsales@wwnorton.com or 800-233-4830

Manufacturing by Bradford & Bigelow
Book design by Bytheway Publishing Services
Production manager: Leeann Graham

Library of Congress Cataloging-in-Publication Data

Wexler, David B., 1953–
   [Stop domestic violence]
   The stop domestic violence program : innovative skills, techniques, options, and plans for better
relationships : group leader's manual / David B. Wexler, Ph.D. — Third edition, revised and updated.
        pages   cm. — (A Norton professional book)
   Includes bibliographical references and index.
   ISBN 978-0-393-70870-7 (pbk.)
   1. Wife abuse—Prevention—Handbooks, manuals, etc.   2. Abusive men—Rehabilitation—
Handbooks, manuals, etc.   3. Group psychotherapy—Handbooks, manuals, etc.   I. Title.
HV6626.W44 2013
362.82'9254—dc23   2013005129

W. W. Norton & Company, Inc., 500 Fifth Avenue, New York, N.Y. 10110
www.wwnorton.com
W. W. Norton & Company Ltd., Castle House, 15 Carlisle Street, London W1D 3BS

2   3   4   5   6   7   8   9   0

Contents

Introduction and Acknowledgments

When I train people to run meaningful and effective domestic violence treatment groups, I conclude the workshop by making sure they know they are embarking on a sacred mission.

The violence and abuse that cripples way too many families generates this mission. Any step we can take—any step—saves someone and points to a better future for all families. The mission of this newly upgraded third edition of *The STOP Program* is to offer a clearer path toward engaging the people who commit acts of abuse and violence so that they can change and commit less abuse and less violence. It's as simple as that.

This new edition of *The STOP Program* reflects our ongoing integration of new research, creative interventions, and pure trial-and-error findings. Here are some of the key updates:

1. I have included new sessions with the following themes:

   Effect of trauma on domestic violence (specifically several new interventions focusing on the connection between posttraumatic stress disorder and domestic violence)

   Imaginary crimes, survivor guilt, and domestic violence

   "Negative interpretations" (based on research about aggressive and criminogenic attitudes)

   Guidelines for "good men"

   Mindfulness and gratitudes (based on contemporary research about generating positive affect and attitude—there is one session devoted to this plus exercises at the beginning of every session)

   Intimacy training (several new sessions with new skills for empathy, revealing personal information, etc., including the new *Relationship Respect Contract*)

2. Because of the success of using video clips to generate structured discussion about specific topics, I have added scenes from the following four movies:
   Boyz 'N the Hood
   Ordinary People
   Tough Guise
   The Hurt Locker

3. I also included new and updated background material for group leaders to enhance their skills, including the following articles:

"Shame-o-Phobia"

"Approaching the Unapproachable—Therapist Self-Disclosure to De-shame Male Clients"

"What Men Want From DV Groups"

4. Finally (based on innovative new trends in treating substance abuse issues concurrently with domestic violence), I have included a supplementary program to integrate a Level II substance abuse focus into domestic violence treatment, when indicated. This option will be invaluable to programs that need to address these issues together.

Finally, once again, thanks to all the men who have been willing to take risks and face tough issues in their lives. Many of these men now feel like they are on a mission of personal growth and relationship health. We join them on this mission.

David B. Wexler, Ph.D.
www.RTIprojects.org
November 2012

Introduction and Acknowledgments to the Second Edition

In this field, you have to stay fresh. The work is too important, and the consequences of missteps too tragic, to stand still.

When men were accused of domestic violence prior to the 1970s, it was usually considered a "family thing." Unless it was too serious to ignore, police typically looked the other way, nobody identified the problem as a significant social issue, and no substantive programs existed to identify the problem, treat the abusers, and offer support for the victims.

With breathtaking speed and innovation, the feminist movement insisted on drawing attention to this issue and identified partner abuse as an issue of gender politics that required consciousness-raising for men and support for women. This wave of attention led to the development of women's shelters, men's groups to challenge the attitudes and behavior of male abusers, and the development of specialized units in police departments, courts, and probation departments. At least in the more progressive states and counties, domestic violence charges were taken seriously, and programs were established to address the tragic cost of these behaviors. Male relationship violence was identified as part of a larger pattern of sexist attitudes, male entitlement, and men using aggression to get their way when they felt like it. The driving force of all male relationship violence was targeted as "power and control." Violent women were almost identified as acting in self-defense. Programs to rehabilitate male abusers were considered to be educational in nature to "re-program" male attitudes and expectations in relationships.

And now, with deep gratitude to those who demanded attention and re-thinking of these issues, we continue to move forward. Men abuse women plenty, but some women abuse men as well. We now know that "one size does not fit all": Only a minority of male domestic violence represents true battering, or "intimate terrorism," while the majority (both male and female) instead represents "situational couple violence." While the "power and control" theme still drives some of the most disturbing male abuse, many men are simply driven more by poor skills deficits in managing the complexities of emotionally intimate relationships.

Most important for our purposes here and for your purposes in treating those men who have abused their female partners, we now know that the best way to "rehabilitate" these men is not by branding them as "batterers" or by demanding that they identify their behavior as driven by "power and control" themes. The trends in the field now inform us that the best way, simply, is to offer respect to these men as men. While always insisting on full accountability for behavior, we need to recognize their own profound sense of powerlessness in relationships and help equip them with better models for making sense of relationship problems and a wider range of emotionally intelligent skills for responding to them. We need to honor their perspective, at times, that their female partners often engage in violent behavior that is not strictly self-defense. We need to equip them with tools for handling relationship conflicts more successfully—based on the assumptions that most men actually want this, rather than the assumption that most men actually don't.

And in so doing, we aim to accomplish our mission of helping these men become the best men they can be and to reduce—ideally, to eliminate—the likelihood of relationship violence in the future. This is the mission of the STOP Program, improved and upgraded and newly informed by the flood of research and new models in this field.

Those of you who are already familiar with the Domestic Violence 2000 program will recognize many familiar themes—and many new ones. By the time you read this, and by the time you start using the STOP Program for a while, it will again be time for something new (especially "matching typology to treatment": different programs designed for different types of domestic violence offenders). So I encourage you to use the STOP Program—but don't get too comfortable!

The original development of the STOP Program treatment model for domestic violence emerged from a collaborative effort as part of a research project evaluating military domestic violence treatment programs, co-sponsored by the Department of Defense and the National Institute of Mental Health. The research was conducted by a team from the University of Colorado, headed by principal investigator Franklyn W. Dunford, Ph.D., of the University of Colorado, who offered sage counsel and impeccable support to the fine-tuning of this program. I would like to particularly express my gratitude to the U.S. Navy Family Advocacy Program administrators and staff throughout the years for offering so much support and invaluable creative contributions to this body of work.

Daniel G. Saunders, Ph.D., was a primary consultant and contributor to this treatment program from the outset. Some of his specific contributions are noted in the text, but many of his informal contributions are not. He has brought vast experience in the field of domestic violence treatment and the highest standards of professionalism to our programs and this manual.

I would also like to thank the clinical consultant staff of the Relationship Training Institute, who have been providing outstanding clinical services for the Navy Family Advocacy Center in San Diego since 1986. Their contributions to the program and to the refinement of this manual have been outstanding. I would particularly like to thank James A. Reavis, Psy.D., for his significant contributions. In recent years, the clinical staff has included Daniel Blaess, Ph.D.; Sage De Beixidon Breslin, Ph.D.; Stacy Buhbe, Ph.D.; Dennis Harris, MFT; and Karen Hyland, Ph.D. Their expertise and passion for this work have contributed to the program you see here in immeasurable ways. I would also like to offer special thanks to Cynthia Martin, Ph.D., and Karen McCardle, MFT, for their passion for baseball and for offering so much to the work we do.

The San Diego Domestic Violence Council and the coordinated community efforts of city attorney, district attorney, police department, judges, community agencies, and victim support groups have provided an extremely fertile climate for the development of these ideas.

Many thanks also to my mentors and heroes in this sacred work: Donald Dutton, Amy Holtzworth-Munroe, Jackson Katz, Don Meichenbaum, Bill O'Hanlon, John Gottman, Terry Real, Bill Pollack, and Ron Levant.

Finally, thanks to all the men who have given so much of themselves and worked so hard throughout our years of treatment. We have found that men who commit acts of domestic violence come in many shapes and sizes and that each man has a unique story to tell.

The STOP Domestic Violence Program

THIRD EDITION, REVISED AND UPDATED

PART I
FOUNDATIONS

PROGRAM NOTES

The STOP Program, Third Edition, is the new, improved, and modernized version of the *Domestic Violence 2000* program published in 1999 and *The STOP Program* published in 2006. This new edition of *The STOP Program* is specifically designed for programs that have 52 weekly group sessions, but the 26-session format also makes it suitable for programs with 26 weekly sessions (and many programs adapt the STOP Program in settings, such as the military, which only allow for shorter program lengths). The program integrates elements from profeminist, cognitive-behavioral, and self-psychological models for treating domestic violence. The program format and message insist that men examine the dominance and control aspects of domestic violence—especially issues of male entitlement and privilege. It offers men intensive training in new skills for self-management, communication, problem solving, and empathy for others. And group counselors consistently employ a client-centered approach that emphasizes respect for the men's experience—both in personal history and in present relationships—as well as empathic understanding of why men choose to act the way that they do. The approach is political, educational, and psychological. This model had been carefully constructed through 30 years of trial and error and through paying attention to input from new research in the field.

Each decade there is so much more that we know about how domestic violence takes place and about what works in treating it, and *The STOP Program, Third Edition,* integrates this new information.

1. **PROGRAM DESIGN:** This manual is designed for use as part of an open-ended 52-week treatment program for male domestic violence offenders, but the 26-session format also makes it suitable for programs with 26 weekly sessions.

2. **SESSION STRUCTURE:** Each session is designed for a 2-hour period, with a 10-minute break in the middle. Also, please note that all group sessions begin with review of homework from the previous session, plus a brief mindfulness and gratitude ritual, followed by a review of the *Weekly Check-In* (see the *Standard Forms* section), which each group member must fill out prior to the beginning of group. The group leaders should briefly review these check-ins to alert them to any specific issues, which should be covered in that session.

3. **HANDOUTS:** The group members use *The STOP Program: Handouts and Homework*, which includes the forms, exercises, and homework assignments for the sessions as well as the additional material.

4. **TEACHING METHODS:** These sessions are designed to be psychoeducational, with lectures, demonstration, role playing, and personal group discussion. Both the educational and the psychological are essential for the program's success. In order for group members to properly learn the skills and techniques, group discussion of personal experiences and specific applications is encouraged.

5. **EVALUATION FORM:** The *Evaluation Form* that you will be using to evaluate group members' performances should be previewed at intake with each group member. Explain each of the criteria. It is also helpful to review these items in the group format. As you review each item, ask at least one group member to assess his own performance in this area. This is an excellent opportunity to offer genuine feedback, bolster self-esteem, and stimulate increased mutual support from group members.

6. **HOMEWORK:** Homework is regularly assigned throughout these sessions. All homework should be reviewed early in each session. It is not necessary (and too time-consuming) to carefully review each group member's homework each session. However, it is essential to at least review one or two examples of the homework and to conduct a quick visual check to make sure all group members have completed the work. Group members will quickly recognize if homework is not taken seriously and thus they will not take it seriously.

7. **ORIENTATION SESSIONS:** Several forms are included for meeting with new group members prior to their first group session. Research has indicated that this pre-group preparation is extremely valuable in setting the stage for successful treatment.

8. **NEW MEMBER SESSIONS:** When new members are entering the group, the model for *The STOP Program, Third Edition,* is to engage in a brief "getting to know you" exercise (described in the *New Member Session* information) and to review one of two exercises with the group: *House of Abuse* or *Time-Out.* In other words, if you review the *House of Abuse* in a new member session in January, you will review *Time-Out* in February, and then *House of Abuse* again in March, and so on. This information is so central to our work that it bears repeating for the veteran group members, who actually "get it" better and better with every repetition.

   The material for a new member session is not a replacement for the scheduled material in the sessions. It should be integrated into the overall format of that session as much as possible.

   If possible, new group members should only be admitted during one session each month. In other words, there will be one session per month in each group during which new members will be integrated; the remaining sessions each month will not be disrupted by new admissions.

9. **EXIT SESSIONS:** When an individual group member is within two sessions of completing his program, he should go through the first *Exit Session* exercise (*Most Violent and/or Most Disturbing Incident*). At his final session, he should review his *Prevention Plan*. All group members will thus have witnessed a number of these successful "graduations" by the time it is their turn.

   The material for the exit sessions is not a replacement for the scheduled material in the sessions. It should be integrated into the overall format of that session as much as possible.

10. **STANDARD FORMS:** Several standard forms are included for use in the programs. Each form may be used as is, adapted for the needs of the particular program, or abandoned completely. The key forms are the following:

    Weekly Check-In
    Evaluation Form

11. **THE 15 COMMANDMENTS OF STOP:** *The 15 Commandments of STOP* (see the relevant handout) are central themes that run through all the treatment sessions, even if there are no specific lectures devoted to them. A poster-size version of these commandments should be displayed on the group room walls. Whenever a subject related to any of the commandments emerges in the group discussion, it is helpful to interrupt, point to the poster, and ask someone to read aloud the relevant commandment. The *15 Commandments of STOP* are carefully reviewed in the initial Orientation session.

12. **MALE AND FEMALE CO-FACILITATORS:** The optimal format for leading the groups involves a male and female co-facilitator team. The group members benefit from a counseling relationship with therapists of both genders. We have generally found it valuable for the male co-leader to take the lead when confronting any group members regarding female bashing or negative generalizations about women. This models a different male consciousness about male-female politics—which sounds different when a female appears to be merely defending herself or her gender. The best model, from our experience, is for the male group leader to send the message that even men can be offended by sexism. The co-facilitator team can also effectively model respectful disagreement and conflict resolution.

    Please do not take this as a criticism of programs that run groups with single group leaders or with two men or even two women. These can all work just fine. However, if funding, resources, and personnel allow, then the design of the program is most optimal with a male-female team.

13. **TREATMENT FAILURE (see *Provisional Status Policy*):** If any group member is showing clear signs that treatment is not progressing successfully, he should be confronted about his behavior and informed that there is a problem as early as possible in the treatment program. We usually expect to be able to flag these problems by Weeks Eight or Ten. It is unfair to inform a group member after 37 sessions that we have decided he is not benefiting from the program (unless some unexpected event, like re-abuse, has suddenly taken place). Indications of treatment failure include belligerent attitudes, refusal to do any homework, refusal to participate, consistent verbal aggression when discussing females, and so on.

14. **PROGRAM LIMITATIONS:** When introducing new skills, such as assertiveness, to the group members, it is very important to emphasize that there is no guarantee that these skills will always bring about a positive outcome. In fact, there are times when being "assertive" or using "active listening" or "I-messages" is not the best course. The message we should send is that usually these are the most *respectful* forms of communication, and *respectful* communication is generally the most effective in the long run.

15. **THE *STOP PROGRAM* LIMITATIONS:** Many aspects of conducting a comprehensive domestic violence treatment program are *not* included in this manual,

such as supporting victims, intake and assessment procedures, coordinating efforts with civilian court systems and other agencies, and selecting and supervising staff members. *We strongly recommend that agencies develop thorough systems and policies for the wider range of services in treating domestic violence.* This manual is designed only to treat heterosexual men who have committed some form of substantiated psychological and/or physical act or acts of abuse against their partners.

16. **VIDEOTAPES AND AUDIOTAPES:** Several different DVDs are used in many of the sessions:

- *The Great Santini* is available for purchase from many DVD outlets.
  - High school basketball game begins at 1:03:22 and ends at 1:12:18
  - Father-son one-on-one basketball game begins at 31:48 and ends at 40:23
  - Kids witnessing spouse abuse begins at 1:28:29 and ends at 1:29:57
- *Men's Work* is available from the Hazelden Foundation (1-800-328-9000 or http://www.hazelden.org).
  - Series of put-downs and masculinity challenges begins at 2:07 and ends at 11:57
  - Spaghetti dinner scene begins at 19:16 and ends at 20:20
- *Tough Guise* is available from MediaEd (http://www.mediaed.org).
  - "Men in media" and "Smoke Signals" scenes begin at 10:15 and end at 14:29 (Chapters 6–8)
- *Affliction* is available for purchase from many DVD outlets.
  - "Halloween" scene begins at 13:40 and ends at 19:20
- *Good Will Hunting* is available for purchase from many DVD outlets.
  - "Shame" scene begins at 1:22:43 and ends at 1:27:14
- *Boyz 'N the Hood* is available for purchase from many DVD outlets.
  - Father-son scene begins at 1:32:29 and ends at 1:37:28
- *The Hurt Locker* is available for purchase from many DVD outlets.
  - "Vets returning home" scene begins at 1:57:20 and ends at 2:05:51 (Chapters 17–18)
- *Ordinary People* is available for purchase from many DVD outlets.
  - "Survivor guilt" scene begins at 1:36:08 and ends at 1:45:39

The exact timing of the specific video clips may vary on different DVD players.

Program co-facilitators are strongly encouraged to use their own video clips to specifically illustrate key points in this program. However, only brief video clips should be used—group members should never be stuck in a room to watch a 1-hour or 2-hour video. This is not the best use of group time.

RULES OF ENGAGEMENT

Assumptions

1. All of us working in the field of domestic violence treatment and prevention recognize that we have one primary mission: to reduce the likelihood—ideally, to eliminate—the risk of future relationship violence.

2. Programs like the STOP Program are committed to targeting the men (or women) who have been identified as perpetrators of relationship violence, and doing everything we possibly can to have a positive impact on how they conduct themselves in the future. Our goal is one of rehabilitation and change.

3. In working with men (or women) who have committed these acts of relationship violence, our most effective strategy is to "engage" the group member to increase the likelihood that he or she will be receptive to change. If we don't reach them, we can't change them.

Communicating Respect

It is often difficult for group leaders to listen to the stories of the men in our program dispassionately and compassionately. We all enter this setting with our own values and judgments—let alone personal experiences—and the process of understanding a man who abuses his partner can provoke difficult emotions.

The men in this program deserve our respect—not, obviously, for the actions they have taken, but rather for the individual stories that have led them to act desperately and destructively. It is very helpful to recognize that many of the men in our groups—*like all of us*—have become overwhelmed by emotions that they had difficulty handling. And they have lacked the necessary range of skills to handle these emotions in constructive and proactive ways. Although we must always emphasize personal responsibility, it is also essential to recognize our essential similarity and their essential humanity.

It is our belief that when these men become smarter about themselves (more aware of needs, feelings, and motivations) and smarter about options (better skills at self-talk, relaxation, communication, empathy, and problem solving), they will choose to act otherwise in the future.

PACING AND LEADING (see the *Pacing and Leading* guidelines): One treatment strategy to help facilitate these goals is called "pacing and leading." This approach employs the process of carefully *mirroring* or *pacing* the experience of the other person, followed by a *leading* suggestion for a new way to think or act.

This sequence of communicating empathic understanding and respect for the man's experience and then offering a new perspective or idea proves very valuable in these groups.

LABELING: It is vital to communicate this message: *We treat the man, not the label.* Stay away from labels that sound like put-downs, such as *batterers, perpetrators, abusers,* and so on. They may be true, and they may be the labels in the legal system, but they do nothing but foster shame—and resistance. We want the men to understand that we could put any man in this group, regardless of what has gone wrong in his relationship patterns, and he would benefit from the approaches used in this treatment model.

REFRAMING NEGATIVE EMOTIONS: It is both respectful and productive to reframe negative emotions such as jealousy, hurt, and disrespect as signs of attachment: *If you didn't care about her, and what she thinks of you, this wouldn't matter so much.* Of course, this cannot be the only perspective on these emotions, but they do allow the men to examine these emotions without automatically coming to extreme negative conclusions about themselves, their partners, or their relationships. It is also valuable to help them apply this same perspective to the negative emotional states of their partners.

INITIAL RESISTANCE: Very frequently group members enter the first group session angry and resistant. They complain about being in the group, challenge the group policies, and insist that they will not be speaking or participating. Unless they are seriously disruptive to the group, it is usually best to respectfully listen to their complaints and then move on. **Power struggles should be avoided whenever possible**. Often men who are the most difficult in the early sessions turn out to be the best group members—as long as they have initially felt respected.

TAKING THINGS SERIOUSLY: Often, the group members will become uncomfortable with the emotionally disturbing discussions that emerge in the group—and they deal with this by laughing or making fun. Sometimes this happens when a group member describes some act of violence toward his wife or partner that he delivered because she was nagging him so much. It can get tiring for the group leaders to "lecture" the group about how "this is not a funny subject." Often, modeling has the most impact. The group leaders should simply maintain a serious tone. The group members usually get the message quickly. Many of these men are surprisingly sensitive to social cues about correct behavior and they don't want to "look bad" in front of others.

SYSTEM BASHING: System bashing also occurs frequently in the groups: Men will speak negatively about the court system, Child Protective Services, and child custody laws. These discussions should be short-circuited as quickly as possible. Unlike women bashing, however, it is rarely effective to confront these complaints. For one thing, the men may be justified in their complaints. For another, it is unproductive to engage in any unnecessary power struggles. The most effective strategy seems to be saying something like this: *You know, you may be right about some of your complaints, but this isn't really the focus of the group sessions. What we need to talk about here are the things* you *can do differently.*

WOMEN BASHING: "Women bashing" often occurs in these group sessions. In contrast to "system bashing," this should be confronted **immediately**. Group leaders should point out that generalizations about any social group always turn people into categories rather than individuals. It should be emphasized that *it's okay to say that your wife complains a lot but not to say that all women are nags.* Furthermore, men who refer to their wife as "the wife" or "she" or even "my wife" should be consistently asked to refer to her *by name.* It can be "humanizing" to write the name of each of the "women" in the group on the board as their names come up during each session. Our goal is to make the women in these men's lives as real and human as possible.

POWERLESSNESS AND ACCOUNTABILITY: Although it is obvious that dominance and control are central themes for many of the perpetrators, it is also important to recognize how *powerless* many of these men feel. When we can identify this experience of powerlessness, many of these men are much more accessible to us. They feel less blamed as bad people and more understood as men who have been frustrated or have felt wounded. **It is quite possible to communicate this message without absolving men of responsibility for their abusive actions.** Consider this message: *We want you to take 100% responsibility for your own behavior but not necessarily 100% blame for all the problems.*

A User-Friendly Environment

Not only is it important to engage the group members by communicating respect, but this atmosphere of respect is also communicated through the structure of the program and the treatment environment that we design for them. It is also important to recognize the learning styles of the men in our groups and design interventions accordingly.

SHAME-FREE GROUP NAMES: Domestic violence treatment groups should not be called domestic violence treatment groups, at least not as far as the group members are concerned. The names should be neutral, like *Group HAWK* or *Group EAGLE,* or positive, like *Relationship Skills Training* or *The STOP Program.* These men are very sensitive to being and feeling shamed about their behaviors, and the shame experience rarely makes them more amenable to change. Instead, it generates defensiveness and resistance.

"SHAME-FRIENDLY" GROUP ENVIRONMENT: The discussion in the group should not lead to more shaming than they are already experiencing. Challenging the group members to recognize the ways in which their behavior has been abusive is one thing; communicating disgust is another. There needs to be room for them to discuss their feelings of shame about their behavior without feeling more of it. The goal is to create a "shame-friendly" group environment in which shame can be identified and integrated.

INTERACTIVE, ENGAGING TECHNIQUES: Another important design issue for these programs is to make sure that the information that is so vital for the men's progress is presented in ways that are engaging and user-friendly. Lectures need to be simple and straightforward. The use of video clips, group exercises, demonstrations and role playing, and humor all enhance the attention span and receptivity of our audience.

COUPLES' TREATMENT OPTIONS: Many state statutes prohibit any couples treatment options, at least until the offender has fully completed his or her own treatment program. In many cases, this policy makes sense. However, many of the men in our programs know that their partners have also significantly contributed to the violence at home. Even if it is not used in a particular case, the awareness among group members that couples' treatment is available communicates the message that the program understands the complexity of many domestic violence situations.

MINORITY-SPECIFIC GROUPS: Again, this may not be possible at all sites and many programs may object to this on theoretical grounds. However, sometimes men of various minority groups (African American, Mexican American, Filipino, gay, etc.) feel more comfortable and can be more open in these homogeneous groups.

The Therapeutic Alliance

Another obvious issue in generating the engagement experience revolves around specific interventions to foster a therapeutic alliance. Years of research about the efficacy of clinical interventions in any setting have taught us that this variable is one of the most essential contributors to any treatment success.

Often this alliance is generated naturally, if the counselor has an intuitive sense of how to foster alliance and if the group members are receptive. Most of you working in this field are already skilled at this. The brief list of ideas below is intended to remind you of some specific approaches that may enhance this alliance even further.

UNIVERSAL EXPERIENCE: It is very valuable for group members to hear the basic message that **"anybody could benefit from this program."** In other words, these men are not criminal freaks. They are men who—like many of us—have failed sometimes in handling the complexities of love relationships. Without in any way minimizing the seriousness and tragedy of their offenses, it is still very treatment-friendly to make it clear that the group leaders, too, could benefit from going through a program like this that examines relationship assumptions and relationship behaviors.

PRE-GROUP PREPARATION: As Yalom (1995) has indicated, one of the most valuable contributors to the success of "brief" group therapies is the use of appropriate pre-group preparation. This helps foster the alliance, right off the bat, that is necessary for successful group performance. The Orientation session of the STOP Program is designed with exactly these principles in mind. We want to have the new, unsure, and defensive group member form an alliance with the group leader(s) without dealing with any competition from the rest of the group.

TYPOLOGIES OF DOMESTIC VIOLENCE OFFENDERS
One Size Does Not Fit All

"Who are these guys?"

Recent research in the field of determining different types of domestic violence offenders has yielded valuable insights into how and why domestic violence takes place. The research has been conducted almost exclusively on adult male heterosexual offenders and should not automatically be applied to domestic violence offenders who are adolescent, female, or gay. We know now that the men who commit these acts have a wide variety of motivations, triggers for aggression, personal histories, and personality styles. And they operate in different kinds of relationships.

This brief review is simply a brief review—it is not intended to be comprehensive for all the different research and theory in this field. In the years of developing *The STOP Program, Third Edition,* I have particularly found the research of Michael Johnson at Penn State University (2000, 2008) and Amy Holtzworth-Munroe and colleagues (1994, 2000) at Indiana University to be invaluable. This research and other contributions will be reviewed here.

Similarities

While we now know how different domestic violence offenders are, it is also important to first summarize the factors that they have in common. Here's what the research tells us:

- Hold attitudes that evaluate the use of force less negatively
- Distort causes and consequences of behavior
- Assume greater partner negative intent
- Less able to use reasoning
- Higher levels of arousal in response to conflict
- Higher generalized anger/hostility
- Label many forms of negative affect (hurt, jealousy, fear) as anger
- More likely to be unemployed
- More likely to abuse substances
- More likely to have witnessed family violence as a child

Typologies and Differences I

Research by Johnson (2000, 2008) has indicated distinctively different profiles of perpetrators of domestic violence. This research identifies the category of "intimate partner terrorism" (formerly known as "patriarchal terrorism") as representing a very different set of motivations, personality type, and quality of relationship than the category of "situational couple violence" (formerly known as "common couple violence").

INTIMATE PARTNER TERRORISM

"Intimate partner terrorism" describes domestic violence in which the primary abuser is almost always male, the abusive behavior is usually more frequent and severe, and the primary abuser systematically "coercively controls" the partner.

SITUATIONAL COUPLE VIOLENCE

"Situational couple violence" describes domestic violence in which the violence may be initiated equally by women and men and it is *not* characterized by a pattern of "coercive control."

Johnson (2000) reports that some intimate terrorism actually involves only a low level of physical violence. The distinguishing feature of intimate terrorism involves a general motive to control. The controlling behaviors of intimate terrorism often involve emotional abuse that can gradually alter victims' views of themselves, their relationships, and their place in the world. This pattern of psychological abuse results in victims who become demoralized and trapped in abusive relationships.

Typologies and Differences II

Holtzworth-Munroe (2000) identified four types of male domestic violence offenders. The categories are based on assessment of frequency, severity, and generalization of violence, as well as key personality variables (such as antisocial traits, anger, depression, anxiety, jealousy, and fear of abandonment).

GENERALLY VIOLENT AGGRESSOR (GVA)

GVA batterers have early experiences that increase the risk of developing positive attitudes toward violence and negative attitudes toward women while failing to develop social skills in intimate or nonintimate situations. Their relationship violence is simply a part of their general pattern of violent and criminal behavior.

- generally antisocial and more likely to engage in instrumental violence
- tend to be violent across situations and with different victims
- more generally belligerent
- more likely to abuse substances
- more likely to have a criminal history
- more likely to have been the victim of child abuse
- more likely to have witnessed spouse abuse
- show little remorse
- limited in their capacity for empathy and attachment
- extremely negative attitudes toward women and conservative views of relationships
- high pattern of inflicting psychological and sexual abuse

- high association historically with deviant peers
- attitudes supportive of violence

Items on the *Millon Adult Personality Inventory* (Millon, Millon, Davis, & Grossman, 2006) that contribute to this category include the following:

- *I got in trouble as a teenager.*
- *I have used illegal drugs.*
- *I have done impulsive things that have got me in trouble.*
- *Punishment doesn't stop me from getting in trouble.*

FAMILY-ONLY (FO)

The use of physical aggression emerges as a result of poor partner-specific communication skills, dependence on and preoccupation with the partner, and mild problems with impulsivity.

- little or no significant evidence of psychopathology
- mild social-skill deficits
- moderately dependent and jealous
- passive and passive-aggressive style
- overcontrolled hostility: tend to suppress emotions and withdraw, later erupting into violence after long periods of unexpressed but seething rage
- acts of abuse are generally less severe
- generally remorseful about their actions
- least likely to be violent outside the home
- least psychologically abusive
- most liberal attitudes toward women (when compared with other types)
- low levels of anger, depression, and jealousy, but high on "impression management"
- least likely to have been abused as children

LOW LEVEL ANTISOCIAL (LLA)

Low Level Antisocial is the category generated by the research for men whose characteristics overlapped the GVA and FO categories. They do not reach the full criteria levels for GVA, but they have enough GVA characteristics so that they cannot be appropriately classified in the FO group. This category does not have a set of descriptive criteria independent of the two categories above.

BORDERLINE/DYSPHORIC (BD)

Emotionally dysphoric/borderline domestic violence offenders, when confronted with relationship conflicts, typically perceive them as threats of abandonment. Lacking the skills to resolve such conflicts, they impulsively use physical aggression to express their distress and intense anger.

- high scores for psychopathology, impulsivity, and aggression
- experienced parental rejection and child abuse
- emotionally volatile

- tend to be violent only within their family
- more socially isolated and socially incompetent than other batterers
- exhibit the highest levels of anger, depression, jealousy, and fear of abandonment
- find ways of misinterpreting their partners and blaming their partners for their own mood states
- depression and feelings of inadequacy are prominent
- most severely abused as children

Items on the *Millon Adult Personality Inventory* (Millon, Millon, Davis, & Grossman, 2006) that contribute to this category include the following:

- *I create situations where I then feel hurt or rejected.*
- *I will do something desperate to prevent abandonment.*
- *Being alone frightens me.*
- *Most people think poorly of me.*

THE CONTEXT OF COMPETENCE

Generating the "context of competence" is an approach based on principles for solution-focused therapies (O'Hanlon & Weiner-Davis, 1989). Based on the original work of Milton Erickson, these solution-focused approaches insist on emphasizing the inherent strengths in the individual or in the family system, rather than focusing exclusively on deficits, problems, or failures. The philosophy of the "context of competence" is to "catch yourself doing something right." Even when people have made mistakes or behaved destructively in their relationships, it is very valuable to still identify the parts that went right—and to build on these strengths.

This is a problem-solving approach to difficulties that concentrates more on finding effective ways to meet challenges rather than analyzing all the reasons why someone finds himself in these difficulties (which can be very interesting but generally does not bring about change). It can be applied to a wide range of problems and challenges, and it is not limited to any one theoretical approach.

Even if you never use any of the specific techniques or strategies of solution-focused therapies in your group programs, it is extremely valuable to help create the "context of competence" atmosphere. Many of the men in our domestic violence programs experience intense levels of shame and failure. This is not an excuse for abuse—it is just a psychological reality. If our dominant goal is to prevent future relationship violence, then one of our most valuable strategies is to help bring out their best qualities—using whatever it takes to help them get there.

Essentially, we are sending the men the message that we believe they are fully capable of handling their relationships more successfully. We want to identify those successes very clearly and reward them for doing things right while never, of course, minimizing or ignoring the things they do wrong.

Even the very first question on the *Weekly Check-In* about reporting weekly successes is a direct reflection of the "context of competence" orientation.

In analyzing a relationship problem, it is also very helpful to identify the strengths that already exist.

> PAST SUCCESS: *What have you done in the past that was successful?*
> POSITIVE EXCEPTIONS: *Even though you argue a lot about money, when are you able to talk about money <u>without arguing</u>?*
> COPING STATEMENTS: *What do you already know about how to handle these issues successfully?*

SCALING QUESTIONS: *I know you still bicker and criticize each other. But pay attention to times when it's happening less frequently (or doesn't last as long, or never gets as bad as it used to).*

Typical questions that help generate the "context of competence" are the following:

- *How will we know when you've really been successful with the STOP Program?*
- *After you finish coming here, what kinds of changes do you think you'll continue to make in your life?*
- *What's the first sign you'll be able to notice that the STOP Program has been helpful to you?*
- *What's the first sign others will be able to see that the STOP Program has been helpful to you?*
- *If you've experienced similar problems before, how did you deal with it?*
- *Tell us about one of the times when you started to lose it—but you stopped it before it went too far?*
- *Can you remember a time recently when you pleasantly surprised yourself or did something out of character that pleased you?*
- *Even though you yelled at your wife, it sounds like you were able to stop yourself from threatening her or becoming physical. How were you successful at stopping yourself here?*
- *Even though you had a big blowout, it sounds like the two of you were able to end it pretty quickly—and after about an hour it was pretty much over. How were the two of you successful at recovering so quickly?*

PACING AND LEADING

One strategy to bypass the inherent defensiveness of the domestic violence offenders in our programs is called "pacing and leading." This approach, originating from the work of Milton Erickson and further developed by neo-Ericksonian practitioners (Erickson & Rossi, 1979; Gilligan, 1987), carefully mirrors the experience of the other person—followed by a "leading" suggestion for a new way to think or act. Based on Erickson's original work with indirect, naturalistic hypnotherapy, pacing means first developing empathy and rapport for the other person's experience by careful delineation—prior to making any correction or suggestion, prior to fostering a new perspective, prior to guiding a new behavior.

STEP ONE: Offering mirroring responses that confirm the person's experience
STEP TWO: Then—and only then—"leading" him into some new ways of thinking, feeling, or behaving

In domestic violence groups, "pacing" means carefully reflecting back an understanding of the men's experience:

> When Karen was talking to this other guy at the party, you must have felt really threatened, like something very important was being taken away from you.
> And you must have felt betrayed, like "How can she do this to me?"
> Plus it was in front of other people, and your pride was at stake.
> And you felt powerless, probably thinking, "I have to _do_ something about this right now."
> You probably felt it all through your body,
> And it felt awful,
> And you didn't know what to do.
> It makes sense that you would feel this way and that you would feel this urge to try to do _something_ to feel powerful again.

Then, and only then, comes the "lead":

> And at that point, probably the most _powerful_ thing to do would be to remember that you get insecure in these situations and that it doesn't always mean that Karen is _doing_ something to you. And to remember that you have ways to talk to her about it afterwards. You can let her know what you need from her.

There are three kinds of mistakes you can make in "pacing and leading":

IMPROPER PACING: If you tell someone that he must be very anxious right now, and he is not, then the pacing is off-base.

INSUFFICIENT PACING: If you make a few pacing statements and he is still very guarded and mistrusting, it may mean that you need to spend more time with the pacing process.

IMPROPER LEAD: Even though you may have paced very accurately and successfully, your "lead" suggestion may be something that doesn't make sense or feels offensive in some way to the person.

When in doubt, return to pacing. It is hard to go wrong by doing this.

In the situation above, the group leader could have simply stepped in with the obvious "lead"—but without proper pacing, the likely response from the group member would have been something like *you don't know what it's like to have her treat me like this!* Without pacing, you lack emotional credibility. With pacing, the person is more likely to feel understood, and then more receptive to the value of the advice, guidance, or correction.

PROVISIONAL STATUS POLICY (Group Leaders' Version)

The following are grounds for placing a group member on *provisional status* in group treatment (leading to possible termination). These criteria are in addition to activity that takes place outside of the group sessions, such as acts of recidivism, substance abuse problems, other criminal behaviors, or failure to attend group:

1. **Consistently** putting down women or minimizing violence

2. **Persistent** disruptive or oppositional behavior in group

3. **Consistent** projection of blame for relationship problems without self-examination

4. **Consistent** lack of participation in group, including failure to complete homework assignments

5. **Consistent** pattern of "telling stories" (bragging or showing off) about controlling, abusive, or violent behavior with little or no signs of remorse

6. **Consistent** pattern of inappropriate messages on clothing (such as T-shirts with sexist messages)

If the group member is deemed to be appropriate for *provisional status* based on the criteria above or other behaviors deemed to be possible grounds for failure, the following steps should be taken:

1. Discuss these concerns directly with the group member. Indicate exactly what you need to see in the future for him to continue in the program. Indicate when his behavior will be reviewed again (usually 1–3 weeks). Depending on clinical judgment, this discussion can take place privately or in the group itself.

2. Follow up with the group member and give feedback indicating either his success in meeting program standards or informing him that you are recommending termination from the program.

It is our policy to attempt to engage group members in the treatment process and to help them correct unacceptable behaviors if possible. Strategies for intervening when group members are engaging in these behaviors include the following:

1. At first, give the benefit of the doubt and assume ignorance: *You may not be aware of this, but . . .* or *I don't think you realize how this comes across, but . . .*

2. Try to keep the interventions as benign and respectful as possible. Remember that these men are feeling shamed and defensive, and they are often testing us to see what they can get away with.

3. As much as possible, state the rules as clearly and simply as possible. Group members are trained to follow clear and direct orders.

4. Employ *pacing and leading* whenever possible. Make sure that the group member feels that his point is recognized and respected even if you are correcting his behavior. Continue to remind the group members that, although their complaints about their partners, their jobs, or the legal system may be valid, the purpose of this group is to examine themselves.

5. If a problem behavior is developing, catch it as early as possible in the group member's treatment. Patterns of problem behavior should be noted and confronted no later than the fourth or fifth session for the offending group member. For example, make a comment the first time someone talks about the way "all women" are.

6. However, be careful about confronting problem behavior too early. Many of these men need to have room to be defended and oppositional early on and often come around on their own.

7. If you are feeling intimidated by a nucleus of group members who are being disruptive, discuss this with colleagues. In these situations, it is often wise to meet privately with problem group members to enlist their alliance with the group goals and also to issue a general (not aimed at a single person) statement about what you expect from the group.

8. If one member is being difficult, you may choose to discuss this in the group, so that other group members can see that someone is taking charge of the direction of the group. Other group members also may have valuable feedback for this particular group member. However, the strategy for handling these situations is to make clinical, case-by-case decisions.

9. Remember that you are fully empowered to recommend that a group member be terminated from the group. This does not represent a failure of the program or the group leaders.

SHAME-O-PHOBIA
Why Men Fear Therapy*

by David B. Wexler

Several years ago, I was on a family trip, sitting on a bench with my wife in a plaza in Paris. Loaded down with shopping bags, she asked me to grab her purse and carry it over to a new spot across the plaza. That's all. Yet even though I knew I was being stupid, I couldn't do it. The 15 seconds being seen carrying a purse were beyond my capacities as a card-carrying male. My wife looked at me like I was nuts and shook her head in disgust.

So what was my problem? All I could envision were people smirking as they saw me publicly toting that damn purse, all of my hard-earned Guy Points accumulated from my half-century of being male suddenly vanishing without a trace.

Shame may be the least understood dimension of men's inner experience—by both men themselves and the people who live with them. In *Affliction*, Russell Banks's classic novel about the tragedy of masculinity, a ne'er-do-well named Wade Whitehouse plans a special Halloween weekend with his 11-year-old daughter, Jill, who lives with her divorced mother, Lillian. Wade's clumsy efforts to make sure Jill has a good time succeed only in making her feel anxious and out of place, and she winds up pleading with him to take her home. But instead of her distress, what stands out for him is his sense of failure: He's shamed by the fact that she's unhappy.

Eventually, still searching for a way out of the pain, Wade gets into an ugly brawl with his ex-wife and her new husband, after Jill secretly calls them to pick her up. As irrationality, belligerence, and self-destructiveness take over, Wade becomes a good man behaving badly, blinded by the specter of his own shameful failure.

Men who've experienced toxic doses of shame early in life will do anything to avoid reexperiencing it as they grow older. It can originate from family experiences, from peer experiences, or just from the culture at large. A shamed boy becomes a hypersensitive man, his radar always finely tuned to the possibility of humiliation. His reaction to slights—perceived or real—and his ever-vigilant attempts to ward them off can become a kind of phobia. Tragically, the very men who are most desperate for affection and approval are the ones who usually can't ask for it: Instead, they project blame and rejection and perceive the worst in others.

Sometimes the smallest signs of withdrawal of affection will trigger old wounds, and they'll suddenly lash out at those they see as slighting them, even as they're un-

*Adapted from D. B. Wexler, "Shame-o-phobia," in *Psychology Networker, 34*(3), 20–51.

aware of the dark feelings stirring inside them. This is a state of mind that many of us in the field call shame-o-phobia, an endemic condition throughout Guy World.

With their profound fear of appearing weak or—god forbid!—feminine, most men will do whatever it takes to prove their manhood. In one recent study, men were assigned to three different groups and given the task of keeping their hand in painfully icy water for as long as they could. Those who were told that the ability to withstand the discomfort was a measure of male sex hormones and an index of physical fitness showed greater cardiovascular reactivity, reported feeling more performance expectations, and kept their hand in the water the longest. This was in contrast to the group who were told the test was a measure of high levels of female sex hormones and the ability to bond with children, and with the third group, who received no explanation at all.

What does this tell us? The length of time a guy will tough it out with his hand submerged in freezing water depends on whether he thinks his masculinity is in question. For some men, their hand could fall off before they'd risk the shame of not seeming "man enough" to take it.

Women feel shame, too, of course, and much of the emotional experiences for men and women are more similar than not. But there are still some fundamental differences in how men are both hardwired and acculturated that can't be ignored in the therapist's office. Even as infants, boys are more overstimulated by direct eye contact and show less ability to regulate arousal through intimate connection. These infant boys then grow up in a Guy World culture that emphasizes successful performance and deemphasizes reliance on others as a way to self-realize.

Furthermore, evolutionary psychology teaches us that men are wired for procuring and performing (while females are wired for tending and befriending)—a trait that may provide a biological backdrop to the modern male focus on success. Without that, he ain't much—or so he feels.

To ignore the powerful effect of shame-o-phobia is to risk not really "getting" men, even if you happen to be a man yourself. An otherwise benign or mildly embarrassing event—like carrying the purse across the plaza, or a daughter who isn't having a good time at a Halloween party—can overactivate a man's fear that he's failing at some central task of being a real man.

The Broken Mirror

A metaphor from self-psychology, the broken mirror, is particularly helpful in understanding the dynamics of male shame. This sensitivity to shame—to feeling incompetent, not valuable, unloved, unneeded, unimportant—is often governed by the psychological relationships with mirroring-self objects in our lives. It works like this: The response from others serves as a mirror, reflecting an image that governs our sense of well-being. Sensitivity to mirroring-self objects and broken mirrors isn't gender-specific, but men are more vulnerable to experiencing these mirrors as referenda on their performance and personal value. When the mirror image is negative (or is perceived as negative), the reflection can reactivate a man's narcissistic injury and delivers a blow to his feeling of competence. There's no more potent a mirror for a man than the one reflected by his intimate partner. If she (or he, in a gay relationship) is unhappy, he's failed. If she offers even a normal, nonabusive criticism, it's as if she's yelling at him: "You've failed at making me happy." And the shame-o-phobic man, vulnerable to broken mirrors and narcissistic injuries, will hear that message whether it's unintended or not.

A few years ago, I was interviewed on a radio show about the psychological concept of the broken mirror. Afterward, the (male) interviewer said to me off-air: "Damn! Now I get what happened to me yesterday! I came out of the bathroom after shaving and I'd nicked myself a little on the cheek. My girlfriend looked up at me and said, 'What happened to you? That's the second time you've done that this week?' And I just went off. I started yelling at her, and then I stormed off, and our plans for the day were ruined. And it was all because I had a manhood attack. I know she didn't mean anything like that, but that's what I heard. What the hell's wrong with me?"

This man experienced his girlfriend's comments as a stab at his masculinity. It was as if she'd said, "What kind of loser are you that you can't even shave properly? Any man should be able to pull that off!" To a guy whose self-esteem—particularly his masculine self-image—feels vulnerable (this includes most men), this simple interchange, silly as it sounds, can feel like an unbearable assault. My radio interviewer, as best as I could tell, didn't suffer from a narcissistic personality disorder, nor was he particularly outside the norm. He experienced the broken mirror and reacted in ways that are typical, in one form or another, for many of us men.

Men and Therapy

The field of counseling and psychotherapy hasn't done a particularly good job of creating a user-friendly environment for male clients. The problem begins with a lack of awareness about the profound impact of shame-o-phobia and the vulnerability to broken mirrors. Furthermore, there's a mismatch between the relational style of many men and the touchy-feely atmosphere of most counseling and psychotherapy.

Think of what we typically ask a man to do in therapy settings: recognize that something is wrong with him, admit that he needs help, openly discuss and express his emotions, get vulnerable, and depend on someone else for guidance and support—all extremely challenging tasks in Guy World.

Too often therapists—both male and female—try to massage men into being more like women in the ways they express themselves and experience their emotions. So it isn't surprising that only one-third of psychotherapy clients are men. Either men have fewer psychological problems (not likely!), or else many are too turned off by the whole therapy enterprise to seek the help they need. In fact, men usually get therapy only because someone else has insisted on it. When I ask men in an initial therapy session, "What are you doing here?" the answer I hear is "My wife told me I needed to be here." Other times, it may be their boss or their grandmother or their doctor, or even a probation officer. They perceive the decision to use the therapeutic services and the process of using them to be not particularly helpful and not particularly masculine—often even downright threatening. It's our job, as counselors and therapists, to adapt our approach to these realities.

Part of what makes treating men challenging is that they generally don't signal their psychic pain as clearly and straightforwardly as women. In the postfeminist turmoil of shifting relationship dynamics, men have been struggling to find a way to relate intelligently, parent sensitively, and manage their emotional needs with more consciousness and depth. Many of us haven't figured out a way to do all these things and still really feel like men. Author William Pollack describes men's anger as their "way of weeping"—an expression of underlying pain that women would more likely display with tears or more direct expressions of sadness and loss. Men also "weep" by drinking, withdrawing, acting defensive, blaming others, getting irritable, being possessive, working excessively, becoming overly competitive, suffering somatic complaints and insomnia, and philandering.

As therapists, we have two choices: shoehorn men into a process that's traditionally been more user-friendly for females, or reshape what we do and how we present it to better reach male clients.

Rules of Engagement

Men often resist standard therapy because they have a hard time admitting that anything is wrong or, if they think something is wrong, they struggle to identify what it is. Another reason they avoid therapy is that they can't tolerate the internalized stigma—the felt shame—associated with feeling needy, dependent, or incompetent. A third disincentive, even with men who know they need help, is the very idea of sitting in a room, talking out loud about all this touchy-feely stuff; it creeps them out.

Finally, many men are simply confused and anxious about the strange, mysterious, and—for all they know—occult process of therapy. They worry about what they're supposed to say, worry about what might be expected of them, and worry about when, how, or if they should disclose anything too "personal." This is uncharted territory, and they want very specific information and instructions—a kind of user's manual—about just what's going to happen to them, how they should behave, and what exactly this strange "therapist" person intends to do with them. I understand this because I feel exactly the same way in new and unfamiliar situations—I want to have all the parameters laid out before I get into anything, so I don't make a fool of myself. If I'm going hiking in unfamiliar territory, I want maps, I want accounts by other people who've been on this trail, and I want a weather report. And if I'm going with unfamiliar people, I like to have some idea of whether they like to chat a lot or enjoy the hike mostly in silence.

Since men tend to loathe the language of psychotherapy, including the name itself, by all means call it something else in your advertising. You don't even have to call it counseling. You can call it stress management, skills training (including parenting skills and building better relationships), coaching, or consulting. Whatever works to get a man in the door and relax his defenses!

An interesting piece of evidence that selling therapy as an "underpay" works better for men is revealed in a study conducted at three West Coast college campuses by John Robertson and Louise Fitzgerald and published in the *Journal of Counseling Psychology* in 1992. The researchers created one brochure that described the center's counseling services in traditional terms and one that used terms like consultations (rather than therapy) and emphasized self-help, classes, workshops, seminars, and a circulating videotape library. Among the men with a positive attitude toward traditional counseling (assessed by questionnaires about help-seeking), the second brochure made almost no difference. But men who scored higher on traditional masculinity measures, like John O'Neil's Gender-Role Conflict Scale, significantly preferred the alternative brochure and reported that they were much likelier to use these services. This is the audience that we often have difficulty reaching.

Guy Talk

Let's assume a man has walked sheepishly into your office for the first time and mumbled a response to your initial greeting. He doesn't understand the process; can't stand the words *therapist, feelings, issues, unconscious,* and *inner child*; would prefer to be anywhere else in the world; and believes his manhood may be hopelessly compromised just by his presence in your office. What are you going to do to engage his interest and curiosity, lessen his anxiety, and convince him that he might, just might, find something interesting and helpful in therapy?

Before you begin, bear in mind the type of overarching, no shaming message that helps to create a therapeutic alliance with male clients: "You're a good man, and you've been making some mistakes," or "You sometimes act badly," or "You can do better," or "Your kids need you to be an even better model for them. We can work together on this."

How do you explain the goals of therapy in "guy talk"? When I work with men who withdraw or become reactive and belligerent whenever a conflict looms with a spouse or partner, I naturally want to help them react with more maturity and insight. I frame this goal in terms of masculine independence, self-control, and personal agency: "We want you to be really powerful. Not over others, but over yourself." "We want to make sure that the everyday crap that comes up for all of us doesn't control you or provoke you into reactions that aren't good for you or the others around you." "We want you to be in charge, not the stuff outside of you."

It's axiomatic that most men have trouble not only talking about feelings, but openly expressing those feelings, so the next step is to normalize their feeling of discomfort with this feature of therapy.

Clinicians Matt Engler-Carlson and David Shepard, professors at California State University, Fullerton, have developed excellent strategies to disarm male discomfort and resistance. For example, how do you help a man who emotionally freezes when his wife reveals that her previous boyfriend once raped her? If he can't describe his feelings at hearing this news, the therapist can acknowledge the client's anxiety: "It's got to be difficult to talk about feelings in front of a woman who's more comfortable sharing her feelings and a therapist who does this all the time!" If the therapist is male, he can normalize by identifying: "We weren't trained for talking personally about things, were we?" If it looks like the client is failing at the task of offering his partner the emotional connection she's seeking (when all it would take would be to say "I feel so horrible, but I'm so glad you told me this"), the therapist can reframe for positive intentions: "I know you want to feel connected to your wife, but it's just hard to find the right words."

The idea is to send out the good-men-behaving-badly message. In this way, the man—and, maybe more important, his partner—hears that the problem isn't that he's a bastard with a cold heart and no soul. His heart is warm and in the right place, but he doesn't know how to put thoughts and feelings into words and actions.

Therapeutic self-disclosure can be another effective way to reduce avoidance and defensiveness by nipping shame in the bud. You can create an atmosphere of trust and intimacy by offering a carefully calibrated glimpse into your own life—acknowledging that you've experienced some of the same struggles and conflicts. I often tell men stories about times I've yelled at my kids, said nasty things, and stupidly overreacted to them. I tell men about the many times I've stubbornly insisted that my wife and I do something my way without really thinking through how this would affect her. I tell them about times when I've been in therapy and how I've fought with therapists who were telling me things that I took as narcissistic injuries. By showing that even though I'm a therapist I've also had problems, I reassure them that self-revealing will not lose them my esteem or confirm their worst fears of what will happen if they let down their guard. This is destigmatizing.

Respect Resistance and Differences

There's a time and place to point out and confront male resistance and defensiveness, but, at least in the early days of therapy, it's usually much more productive to respect defenses. Typically, when we allow men space to protect their own pride, they don't feel so pressed to perform on demand and, consequently, they become more at ease—and less defensive.

In the beginning of therapy, it's therefore important to give men permission to disclose gradually. It's easy for therapists to get impatient when men take a while to warm up to the counseling experience. Often I'll treat a man who initially minimizes the mistakes he's made, blaming everyone else—his wife, his kids, his girlfriend. I don't mess with this at first, because I know he needs to do this until he feels safer and more confident that he'll get a fair shake in my office.

It's helpful to cultivate the fine art of schmoozing. Men like to feel that the conversation—even in therapy—is "normal." Normal means that the therapist relates in a real fashion, not like a shrink. Normal also means discussing the little events that men talk about, like yesterday's football game, something goofy that happened on the way in to the session, a new contract his company is working on, the latest electronic gadgets. Humor helps, too. There's no reason, of course, not to keep these principles in mind with female clients, but it's especially important with men. The more phobic men are about therapy and emotionally vulnerable, the more important schmoozing becomes.

Since many men feel anxious about what they perceive as the vagueness of the whole therapy process, give them as much concrete information as possible. Tell them exactly how long the sessions are, what the length of therapy might be, the role you can and can't play, and what's expected of them to get therapy right. Offer homework, action plans, and the rationale for using them, since men's needs and learning styles favor direct, clear-cut explanations and instructions. I've found this valuable with almost all the men I see.

Recently, one of my male clients told me that his son had complained that he was making that "angry face" again—and my client had no awareness of it. The instant homework assignment: "Ask everyone in your family to let you know every time they notice your angry face or angry voice, and tell them that this is a direct assignment from your therapist." He understood the rationale: You need feedback to improve performance. And he liked the clarity of the task.

"Relational Dread"

Not all the problems men have with therapy, and the therapy milieu, occur in therapy; they often extend to situations with loved ones and friends. Stephen Bergman, a leading researcher on male psychology, coined the term "relational dread" to describe men's sense of being ill-equipped for the arduous task of discussing feelings and processing relationship issues, even with the people they love most. This dread not only keeps many men out of therapy, but it impairs their ability to connect intimately. How does a therapist, engaging in a quintessentially "relational" practice, reach men who suffer from relational dread?

Let's say a guy's marriage is on the line because he can't even identify his emotions, much less express them, and feels under constant pressure from his wife to do so. You can open the conversation with what might be called a clinical icebreaker, saying, "It's hard to talk about these feelings when, for your whole life, you've kept them to yourself." Or to a man who's really struggling, you might offer a teasing, but empathic, comment like, "Man, aren't you glad you showed up here today?"

Then, because he probably feels ashamed of his inability to offer her what she seems to need, you can give him a little encouragement: "I know you don't feel like you're very good at this and that your wife is disappointed," followed by words of encouragement like, "I'm going to help you figure out how to do this, and I know you can do it."

When guys are terrified that any discussion of feelings or relationship issues with their partners—for example, that dreaded question, "So, what did you talk to your shrink about?"—will turn into unbearable marathon sessions, you can throw them a life preserver. Say to them, "When you talk about this issue at home, set an alarm for 10 minutes. Discussion ends then, no matter what." If even 10 minutes is too long for a man who can't tolerate the inherent lack of structure in "feelings-and-relationship" conversations, teach him some very specific relationship-friendly strategies, like "active listening."

For the man who just goes dumb at the critical moment and can't think of the "right" words when he needs them most—a variant of stage fright—be a coach for him. Try the old Virginia Satir technique of "doubling" (standing right next to him and speaking for him): "I'm really trying to be more of the man you want me to be—I'm just freaked out that I might fail at this. That's why I shut down so much." This shows your respect for the fact that his heart may be in the right place, even though his words aren't. By hearing you do it, he gets a model for how it can be done.

Relational Heroism

Terry Real introduced the term relational heroism in working with men in his book *I Don't Want to Talk About It*. I tell men that, every day, they have an opportunity to give to their loved ones, including their kids, a man who's generous, empathic, and honorable. A man can choose to inform his partner about what he's feeling, rather than just withdrawing or acting out. I call this, or any of a thousand other "unnatural" pro-relationship behaviors, an act of genuine heroism. To choose a path that's hard, unfamiliar, awkward, and even frightening—but which is more in keeping with what really matters to them—takes the kind of courage and resolve that characterizes, well, real men.

What could be more heroic than that?

In one of my men's groups, Robert described a "relational hero" moment that the casual observer might not notice. He and his wife had separated after months of tension and discord. By mutual consent, she'd taken their 6-year-old daughter with her to stay with her family in another state for a couple of months. Then she and Robert decided they were ready to give the relationship another try.

When his wife and daughter arrived back in town on a Greyhound bus, Robert met them at the station. His little girl came running up to him, yelling "Daddy, Daddy, Daddy!" with the kind of gusto that only a 6-year-old girl can generate. He swept her into his arms and hugged her tight, then turned to his wife, who was walking more slowly toward him, to embrace her. She turned away and said she was hurt because she should have been the one he hugged first.

Later Robert described his thoughts at that moment: *What a bitch! What am I supposed to do, not hug my own daughter? I can't believe this shit!* But instead of retaliating and venting, he made a decision to stay calm. He told his wife that he was sorry.

He didn't mean to hurt her feelings. He was really glad to see her. He reassured her, "I really love you, and I'm really happy to see you!"

She paused for a second, then smiled and reached out for him. Just like that, it was over—he'd passed a test. Maybe she shouldn't have reacted as she did to his hugging their daughter first, but that's the way it goes sometimes in all of our imperfect relationships. He can either tell himself he won't put up with it and dig in his heels, or he can try and find some way to reassure her. Robert found a way, and it brought out the best in both of them. At that moment, he was a relational hero.

Men perk up when I implore them to act like heroes or reward them for doing so—rather than simply telling them to be more sensitive or more accommodating.

The Honor of Men

There's a haunting scene from the movie *Good Will Hunting* in which Will Hunting (Matt Damon) and his best buddy, Chuckie (Ben Affleck), talk in characteristically male style about an emotion-laden subject. In passing, Chuckie asks Will about how things are going with his girlfriend, Skylar. Tonelessly and abruptly, Will informs his friend that she's "gone." There's a pause. After a few grunts and monosyllabic responses, Chuckie uncovers the fact that Skylar left Boston for medical school in California—a week ago!

Taking in this information about the sudden, sharp turn in the relationship, Chuckie sips from his can of beer, raises his eyebrows a little, and observes, "That sucks."

The empty spaces in this conversation are deafening. It's hard to imagine an exchange like this between two best friends who are women—especially a week after a breakup in one of their lives! But while Chuckie may not have said much, there's a sense of shared, unstated understanding that resonates deeply. Despite the absence of words and explicit emotion, the audience watching this moment between these friends can feel all the solace and sense of connection being conveyed in the spareness of "That sucks."

When we learn to recognize and honor how men communicate their caring, we'll have a better shot at helping them get relief from unnecessary pain and be able to receive and give more in their relationships. When we respect their defenses, honor their intentions in doing the work, speak to them in Guy Talk, and engage them with therapeutic transparency and self-disclosure, the differences in treating men and treating women diminish dramatically.

As women who are in relationships with men who can reveal their vulnerability know so well, it's extremely rewarding to be part of the process through which a man opens up and finds that he still feels like a man, or even like more of one. A client recently said to me, "I think I'm getting the hang of talking about things I've never talked about before without feeling like a wuss." We can all get better at helping men get there, and it's so worthwhile.

APPROACHING THE UNAPPROACHABLE— THERAPIST SELF-DISCLOSURE TO DE-SHAME MALE CLIENTS

by David B. Wexler

If you are a therapist, you know that men are very sensitive to shame and feelings of incompetence. As a result, we have to do whatever we can to de-shame the therapeutic experience. Otherwise men won't show up. And if they do show up, they won't stay. And if they do stay, they won't be as real as they need to be in order to get something out of the experience.

There are a thousand ways to do this which I and others (Englar-Carlson & Stevens, 2006; Good, 1995; Levant & Pollack, 1995; O'Neil, 2008; Pollack & Levant, 1998; Rabinowitz, 2006; Real, 1997; Wexler, 2004, 2006, 2009) have written about extensively over the past 20 years or so.

One way to disarm typical male shame (and its behavioral cousins: denial, minimization, defensiveness, and avoidance) is by the appropriate use of therapist self-disclosure. I have found this to be invaluable in my work with men.

Therapist self-disclosure, carefully calibrated, can be extremely effective in fostering the therapeutic alliance and helping bring men out of their shell. We can create an atmosphere of increased trust and intimacy by acknowledging that the same struggles and conflicts have taken place in our own lives and in our own relationships. This helps men normalize their experiences.

As clinicians, shame is our enemy here—and therapist self-disclosure often defuses shame. Sometimes this means getting creative and going "out of the box" with what we reveal about ourselves and how we do it.

The Value of Self-Disclosure

A recent review of published studies (Henretty & Levitt, 2010) exploring verbal therapist self-disclosure found that self-disclosure almost always had a positive effect

Wexler, D. B. (2013). Approaching the unapproachable—Therapist self-disclosure to de-shame male clients. In A. Rochlen & F. Rabinowitz (Eds.), *Breaking barriers in counseling men: Insights and innovations*. New York: Routledge.

on clients; that clients had a stronger liking for, or attraction to, therapists that self-disclosed; that clients perceived therapists who self-disclosed as warmer; and—most importantly, for our purposes here—that clients self-disclosed more to therapists that also self-disclosed.

Men often say they remember the personal stories that I have revealed in individual and group sessions more than anything else.

I recently told what I call my "Bicycle Shame" story to Jack, a mid-30s male client who was still living off and on with his parents, had never really developed a career, and had never had a real girlfriend. He was feeling humiliated about trying to change any of these things because he felt like this all should have happened long ago. Here's what I told him:

Like most of my friends, I tried learning how to ride a bicycle at about age 5. They all got the hang of it, but I could never quite pull it off. After a while I gave up because I felt so stupid. When my friends would ride their bikes, I acted like bike-riding was kind of lame—my way of defending myself from shame. I felt more ashamed of this with each passing year.

Finally, when I was about 11, I decided I HAD to learn how to ride a bike. I went off by myself one afternoon and just kept trying it until I finally got it. I caught up quickly, and the history never mattered after that.

Jack nodded and mumbled some polite noncommittal response. I thought I had missed the boat, but at least there was no harm done. Then, a few months later, when he was leaving therapy, he told me, with tears in his eyes: *You know that story you told me about you and the bicycle? That is such a perfect example of what I was feeling. That helped me so much, and I'll never forget it.*

In the books that I have written I reveal a number of personal examples to illustrate male dilemmas and sometimes resolutions. I often have men quoting one of my stories to me in the middle of a therapy session: Those nuggets resonate with them more than my brilliant theories and therapeutic prescriptions. Here's what has finally dawned on me after many years of trying hard to strike just the right tone, use just the right intervention, and implement just the right technique: Sharing more of myself might be the most important work I can do for someone else, and especially for a guy.

The same is true when I teach professional workshops: I can literally feel the crowd awakening when I tell something about myself or my marriage or my family to make my point. The more vulnerable I am, the more their receptors seem to wake up.

When done right, this evens the playing field. Men who are highly sensitized to the hierarchical structure of the therapeutic relationship (with the male client in the vulnerable underdog position) tend to relax the more "real" the therapist gets. When I have done this, I have often seen some of the most defended men quickly engage and open the door to the insight and interventions that our therapy sessions can offer. It's not that they forget that I'm the professional in the room and they're not—it just seems like they don't care about that difference anymore, because the relationship of "man-to-man" (or "parent-to-parent" or simply "human-to-human") has become more prominent.

I recently told what I call my "Paris Purse" story to my client, Andrew, who was struggling with feeling like a "pussy" when he tried to tell his wife about the panic attacks he was having. I wanted to get the point across that we guys are totally capable of ascribing manhood tests to practically anything—and that, once we did this, we were screwed because we felt like we had to stay in this confining box of gender role expectations. Here's what I told Andrew:

Several years ago, I was on a family trip, sitting on a bench with my wife in a plaza in Paris. Loaded down with shopping bags, she asked me to grab her purse and carry it over to a new spot across the plaza. That's all. Yet even though I knew I was being stupid, I couldn't do it. The 15 seconds being seen carrying a purse were beyond my capacities as a card-carrying male. My wife looked at me like I was nuts and shook her head in disgust.

The background to this was that I had recently undergone back surgery and was instructed not to lift heavy bags on this trip. So my wife was doing a lot of the heavy lifting—which contributed to my de-masculinization, of course.

So what was my problem? All I could envision were people smirking as they saw me publicly toting that damn purse, all of my hard-earned Guy Points accumulated from my half-century of being male suddenly vanishing without a trace.

Andrew (and his wife) laughed at the absurdity of my purse-phobia. He told me: *I guess you get it.* I nodded. And I reminded him that a secure man can temporarily carry a purse and can have a real and honest conversation with the woman he loves about his inner world.

Keep in mind that the therapeutic alliance, according to volumes of therapeutic outcome research, is vastly more significant in determining positive treatment outcome than any specific intervention or technique. Measures of therapeutic relationship variables consistently correlate higher with client outcomes than specialized therapy techniques (Lambert & Barley, 2002). This comes as no surprise to students of treatment outcome research in many settings with many different populations over many years.

Often this alliance is generated naturally, if the therapist has an intuitive sense of how to foster alliance and if the male client is receptive. Most therapists are already skilled at this—but it helps all of us to recognize particular strategies that often enhance the therapeutic alliance, thus potentiating the positive effects of treatment.

Enriching this alliance is the central rationale for "out-of-the-box" therapist self-disclosure with male clients. Below I'll illustrate a few key points about disclosing with male clients, with specific examples from my experience and suggestions to consider in your own work.

Types of Self-Disclosure

There are two main types of therapist self-disclosure (Henretty & Levitt, 2010). The first is *self-involving communication (here and now)*, which requires the therapist to express immediate feelings or reactions to the client. For example, when my client Josh told me about how he apologized to his son (for the first time in his life), I said to him, *I am so moved by what you are facing here and the courage it takes to do so.* When my client Daniel slipped into his old familiar pattern of minimizing how his drinking was affecting his family, I stopped and said, *When you talk like this, I feel really worried about you and it's so hard to connect with you.*

This is always a crapshoot: Most men are deeply touched by this more "intimate" response. Others are turned off or downright overwhelmed by the intensity of emotion. There is no specific formula—but keep in mind that the research literature strongly indicates that clients in general (both genders) respond very positively to this level of therapist personal involvement.

The second type, more commonly identified, is *extra-therapeutic* self-disclosure, as in bringing information about yourself into the therapy room that has actually taken place elsewhere: *I got stuck in traffic today* or *I was raised Catholic, too* or *I went skiing with my family last week* or *I have been diagnosed with colon cancer.* All of these, ranging from the banal to the extremely serious, reflect the therapist's decision to reveal something about himself or herself that is otherwise not readily apparent to the client.

The "Twinship" Factor and Passing Tests

The rationale for therapist self-disclosure is best understood by the self-psychology construct of the *twinship* (or *kinship*) selfobject function (Basch, 1988; Shapiro, 1995). According to this model, an individual experiences increased self-cohesion through identification with others. The more that someone feels kindred or has the sense of a shared human experience, the more emotionally integrated and centered he feels. This self-cohesion experience is the essential component of human experience that self-psychology focuses on, and the *twinship* selfobject is (like the *mirroring* selfobject and *idealizing* selfobject and others) one of the pathways that facilitates it.

Another important rationale for the judicious use of therapist self-disclosure requires us to understand how important it for us to pass the male client's tests of us. Control-mastery theory (Weiss & Sampson, 1986; Engel & Ferguson, 1990) is based on extensive research involving detailed observations of psychotherapy sessions. One of the most valuable findings from these studies is that clients often enter psychotherapy (or all relationships, for that matter) with preconceived pathogenic beliefs about themselves, about others, or about how the world works.

According to this model, the client uses the therapy relationship and other intimate relationships to conduct a series of tests. Think of this as an unconscious scientific inquiry in which the client wishes to confirm or disconfirm certain beliefs. In this study, he enters into the investigation expecting to have his original and longstanding pathogenic beliefs confirmed—but he secretly hopes that maybe, this time, they will be disconfirmed.

The old beliefs can change or at least become more flexible. How? By the repeated discovery that, this time, things are different. Or, in some cases, that this time he can handle the situations effectively.

Here's an example. My client Curt was relating an incident when he had screamed at his 12-year-old son in front of his friends when the boy just refused to listen to him. Curt told me this story tentatively—I knew he was (consciously or unconsciously) testing me to see how I would handle hearing this, particularly if I would reprimand or shame him like he was so used to. He was sending up a trial balloon to see how safe it was to reveal so much about himself in our therapy world.

I went for self-disclosure. I told him my "Throwing Joe's Pog Over the Back Fence" story:

My 7-year-old son Joe was not cooperating with me. We had a deal that he would stop playing when I gave him the time warning, clean up his stuff, and get dressed and ready to go wherever it was that we were going. He had plenty of warning. So the time comes around, I let him know it's time, and he just looks at me and keeps playing. I give him a minute, then gently tell him again, no response. We go through this a few times.

Then, as parents tend to do, I started to feel frustrated and powerless and angry. I started the threats. I knew that his most precious possession during that period of his young life was one of his treasured "pogs" (if you don't remember pogs, it doesn't matter—it could have been anything): "If you don't start getting ready in the next 30 seconds, I am going to take away your special pog for the rest of the afternoon." No response. Then it was for 24 hours. Then for the weekend. Then for the whole week.

Finally, in one last desperate attempt to gain control, I pulled out the big one: "If you don't get ready now, I'm going to take your pog and throw it over the back fence into the bushes and you'll never find it again!" When even this didn't move him, I did it. I hurled the pog over the fence. And, of course, he burst into tears.

I don't know exactly what I should have done. But nothing justified what I did. Especially after seeing the look of total betrayal on his face. I am sure that all he took away from this was that his father did a horrible thing.

Curt relaxed. He started telling me even more. I had passed the "equality" test, and he was freer now to own and genuinely examine this part of himself that was capable of destructive behavior.

The HBO show *In Treatment* portrayed a vivid example of a therapist struggling to pass the client's test involving therapist self-disclosure. Sunil, a 50-ish man recently arriving in America from his home country of India, is depressed. His wife of many years has recently died, prompting his son and daughter-in-law to insist that he fly to New York and live with them rather than sink into debilitating depression. They convince him to come to a therapy session to get help with his moods and increasingly erratic behavior.

In the first few sessions, Sunil remains almost mute. He occasionally speaks (in his native language only) to his son, who translates. Then he reluctantly attends a couple of individual sessions, not revealing much.

In his next session, his analytically trained therapist (Paul) invites him to talk more about his grief and depression. Sunil says to Paul, *Where I'm from, when we want to talk, we meet a friend for tea, and then one person speaks and then the other. This is very strange to be expected to do all the talking continuously. . . . I am expected to disclose the details of my life, to speak about my wife, about my pain. . . .* Paul is taken aback. He takes a deep breath, then says, *I did have a wife, but we're divorced now.* (Sunil: *How long were you married?*) *Twenty-one years.* (Sunil: *Do you miss her?*) *Sometimes . . . yes, I do.* Like magic, Sunil starts opening up about his feelings, filling in many details about his history with his wife and his culture and what her loss has meant to him. He goes on, uncharacteristically, for several minutes.

The therapy has started. Why? Because Paul stepped "out of the box" (especially his psychoanalytic training box) and self-revealed more than he would with almost anyone else. He knew that Sunil needed this reciprocity, this level playing field, to open himself up. While Sunil's story comes from a fictional HBO series, this particular scenario is quite realistic and provides all of us with a powerful illustration of the power of getting real (or what Spanish speakers refer to as *personalismo*), particularly for men scared and resistant to the counseling process.

With Sunil, Paul had passed the test. He responded differently than Sunil expected, and genuine therapist self-disclosure was the key.

Self-Disclosure Guidelines

The fundamental caveat of appropriate self-disclosure is this: Only do it when you are pretty damn confident that sharing this information is genuinely in the client's best interest. The potential advantage with male clients is that they are more likely to relax their defenses if they experience a sense of affiliation and kinship rather than distance and inequality. I often tell male clients stories about horrendous blunders I have made with my kids or stupid things I have done or struggled with in my marriage. Sometimes these are humorous, sometimes deadly serious.

I have found these self-disclosures to be absolutely critical in my work with men. Of course, I'm aware of inappropriate self-disclosure or going overboard. And I've definitely erred in this direction at times in my career. But my successes with this far outweigh the mistakes. I've repeatedly found that when I self-disclose it helps de-stigmatize what my client has done or how he feels. It opens up more possibility for them to self-reveal, without the excessive shame that tends to shut them down.

But you can only reveal what you feel comfortable revealing. And if you are not reasonably sure that it will serve a therapeutic purpose (even talking about traffic), then don't do it.

Here are the typical types of self-disclosure that therapists sometimes choose to offer:

> Demographic info (education, theoretical orientation, marital status)
> Feelings and thoughts about the client and/or the therapeutic relationship
> Therapy mistakes
> Relevant past struggles that have been successfully resolved
> Similarities between the client and therapist

The main reasons that any of us would even consider self-disclosure include the following:

> Fostering the therapeutic relationship/alliance and promote client disclosure
> Validating the client's reality
> Normalizing/promoting universality (twinship)
> Offering alternative ways to think or act based on the therapist's experience
> Providing clients with authentic, human-to-human communication

Inappropriate Self-Disclosure

Although it is difficult to establish an absolute set of rules of when to self-disclose and when not to, you may assume that therapist self-disclosure is contraindicated if, in any way, the conscious or unconscious purpose of the self-disclosure is to serve the needs *of the therapist!*

Here are some other specific pitfalls of excessive or inappropriate self-disclosure:

Revealing the "Too Personal": Be careful about revealing information that may place a burden on the client to take care of you or that may lead to a loss of your professional credibility if others in your field found out this same information. You may be tempted to reveal that you too were sexually abused as a child. However, this information may end up getting revealed to others—and it also may lead to the client actually refraining from revealing more, because he doesn't want to re-traumatize you!

Needing a Friend: The reason to self-disclose is to offer something to help the man who is sitting across from you. If you find yourself talking about your recent divorce because you need to talk to someone about it and your client is very interested, you are making a mistake: *I've been going through the same problems with my wife lately, let me tell you about it. . . .* This also can take the form of gossiping: *Yeah, I've heard some real dirt on that other therapist.*

Needing Admiration: Sometimes people in the counseling field, if they are not careful, use their clients to feel admired for personal accomplishments (famous people you know, a book you have published, an important position you have been chosen for): *I had an interesting experience when I was in Milan speaking at the international conference.* Admiring the therapist is not the job of the client.

Losing Credibility: If you think that revealing personal information may actually lead you to lose credibility with your client, then don't do it. I know of a female therapist who was once in an abusive relationship. She almost revealed this to her men's domestic violence group, hoping this self-disclosure would let them know that she knew a lot about this area. But she decided not to—because she suspected (correctly, I believe) that these men would suspect that she could not see them clearly because of her bad experience. Sometimes I choose to reveal that I have been happily married for almost 30 years, to give men some confidence that I know something about making a relationship work—but with some men this signals that I don't know enough about their tormented relationships.

Overreacting to Trauma/Abreaction: When the client is showing a strong emotional reaction to trauma, you cannot allow your own traumatic experiences to emerge. These personal experiences might have been useful in the early stages of the therapy to help you "get a foot in the door" with the client, but now, the focus must be on attunement: bearing the client's traumatic experience together. It is countertherapeutic for the client to recognize that your emotional state is a result of the emergence of your own trauma; the client will be vulnerable to feeling unsafe and ashamed (Carr, 2011).

You may look at these examples and these needs and scoff, certain that you would never make these mistakes. Be careful. No self-respecting, well-trained, non-psychopathic therapist would ever *consciously* use his or her clients to meet these needs or misread a client in these ways. But we all have this potential in us. I know that I have sometimes caught myself slipping some reference into a therapeutic conversation about the success of one of my kids—and then later thought to myself: *How did that ever get into this conversation and what was I getting out of it?* I trust therapists who know that they are capable of this—and who are on the watch for it—more than those who say they are unsusceptible.

Often clients won't tell us when we're self-disclosing too much. They want to be polite, plus they often idealize us and are thus very interested in our lives (even if it has nothing to do with their treatment and is wasting their time by taking care of our needs). For many clients, this may represent an unconscious and unwanted repetition of some very old dysfunctional family patterns.

Self-Disclosure Stories That Help Men in Therapy

Here are a few more stories I tell male clients, in groups or individual sessions. Some of these stories are just at the limit of revealing information about myself that I am not at all proud of—but I have decided I can handle the self-exposure. The ones that are past that limit never see the light of day.

These are my stories, and they work for me because they are my stories—you'll have to find your own. They have to be real (although a little dramatic embellishment is no crime) and they need to reveal some vulnerability on your part. They can be either humorous or deadly serious.

My "Santa Cruz Boardwalk" story is used to illustrate the power and dangerousness of perceived narcissistic injury or what I call "broken mirrors":

It happens to the best of us. One time my 15-year-old daughter sat through a lecture I gave in San Jose, California. I showed a film clip from the movie Affliction *where the main character cops an attitude with his daughter because she is not having a good time at a party he planned for her. Right after this presentation, my family headed off on a drive to the Santa Cruz boardwalk and amusement park. I had been planning this for a long time as a special treat for my kids, and I knew they would like it. My daughter, however, copped her own attitude and complained that this was really kind of boring. I became defensive, and I said to her, "I planned this for you, and it's like nothing's going to make you happy!" She looked at me and calmly said, "Dad, you sound just like that dad in* Affliction.*" I was busted, and she was right.*

I have another story that I call "Calling Off the Wedding," to illustrate the power of messages from fathers to sons—especially messages that positively reframe masculinity:

When I was in my late twenties, I became engaged to a woman whom I had been dating for several years. To make a long story short, we experienced a major crisis several weeks before the wedding and decided to call it off three weeks before the set date. We canceled caterers, bands, and photographers. Family scheduled to fly in from out of town canceled their trips. We returned some presents that had already arrived.

My most intense anxiety, barely second to the pain of this crashing relationship, involved informing my parents, and particularly my father, of this "failure." With the help of a couples therapist who was guiding us, I managed to handle this with some dignity and success. And, although both my parents behaved themselves with grace and came through, I always worried that my father was secretly disappointed in me.

Actually, I didn't even realize that I was still carrying around this worry and shame. But several months later, out of nowhere in the middle of another conversation, my father (not known for being particularly emotionally articulate) turned to me and said, "You know, I don't think I would have had the courage to do what you did when you called off your wedding."

I said thanks. And I remember that moment now, more than 30 years later, like it was yesterday. My father had given me his blessing. He had reframed the decision I had made as one requiring courage rather than one worthy of shame and indicating failure. I probably shouldn't have needed him to tell me that, but we are all human.

Another one that comes in very handy for a male client is my "Surprise Party" story, when I am trying to make the point that he needs to love his partner (or his kids) based on who they really are and what they genuinely need:

My (now) wife and I had been dating for a year and a half. She had told me early on and very emphatically that she was NOT the type of girl who likes surprises: no blindfold dinners, no weekend getaways that she didn't help plan, no surprise parties.

And of course I didn't take her seriously. Her birthday was coming up and I started planning a surprise party. What girl doesn't love a surprise party? And wouldn't I be a great boyfriend if I planned one?

I pulled it off beautifully. All of our friends showed up and she was totally surprised and (apparently) delighted. Until after everyone finally left, when she totally lit into me: "How dare you throw this party when I told you I HATE surprise parties? What do I have to do to get through to you?" And we didn't speak for a couple of days afterward.

It all worked out, because we have now been married 30 years (I add that piece of information very strategically. The meta-message is this: "Good men can behave badly and learn from their mistakes, and good relationships can suffer a serious rupture and still recover"). But I learned an important lesson: The most truly loving thing I can do for my wife is to offer her what she really wants and needs. Not what I think she needs, not what I would need, not what I would want her to need. I have to pay attention to who she is and what means the most to her. That's genuine love. What I did was, ultimately, selfish, more for me than for her.

Conclusion

As therapists, we always need to think pragmatically. In the end, it does not matter (or should not matter) what theoretical orientation we subscribe to or what techniques we employ. The only relevant question is this: Does it work?

With men in therapy, many of our approaches have not always worked, or at least not always worked as well as we would have liked them to. So—when we try to think "out of the box"—we have to keep pursuing approaches that are most likely to attract men, engage men, reassure men, and open the window to helping men access the best qualities in themselves.

If I thought that standing on my head would facilitate this, I would do it (if I could do it). Instead, I have found that the judicious use of self-disclosure (when it is carefully calibrated and quite likely to be in the best interest of the male client) paves the way for reaching men and helping them change.

WHAT MEN WANT FROM DV GROUPS

There will always be some men ordered into a domestic violence treatment group who do not want to be there, who have little or no interest in changing, and who will complain about everything as being unfair or stupid or both.

However, surprisingly, the vast majority of men in these programs actually want to get something out of the experience. Here are some of the typical complaints many men have when a group is not well run (Welland & Ribner, 2010):

- *We get frustrated because we want to change, but they're not giving us enough options and tools.*
- *There's no follow-up from group to group—last week we left off talking about being a father and never followed it up.*
- *The leaders let some of these guys just go on and on about how much they're the victim and how messed up their partners are.*
- *Some of these group leaders spend way too much time on fees and attendance and court documents—sometimes the group doesn't get started until 30 or 40 minutes later.*
- *I've been to some groups where they just stuck us in front of a movie for 2 hours— I could have done that on my own.*
- *The group leader would criticize us a lot; we debated machismo a lot. I think she could have used a better strategy to make us think and debate, instead of the way she did it. Because the way she does it, the men just see her as a "feminist."*
- *It's like these group leaders just have stereotypes of us Mexican men: drunk, womanizer, all that, like they don't have any other picture. They don't know that there are all kinds of men in Mexico, like all over the world, a bit of everything. It was like they were saying it like an attack or a put-down, like despising us. I would have liked them to know the culture with more depth.*

PART II

ORIENTATION SESSION

THE STOP PROGRAM Q&A

 Handout

Welcome to the STOP Program. The following is a list of answers to frequently asked questions about the groups. Please read this information carefully.

1. *Why was I referred to the STOP Program?*
   You were referred to this program because of reports that you were involved in one or more incidents of relationship violence. The fact that you have been referred indicates that this problem is treatable.

2. *How often do the groups meet?*
   Each group meets for 2 hours once a week.

3. *Who else is in the group?*
   The group members include men like yourself who have been involved in some sort of relationship violence. This is an ongoing group. It is very valuable to have group members at different stages of treatment to help explain to you how the group works.

4. *What happens in the group?*
   Our philosophy is that men who get into trouble in their relationships need to learn new skills. We want to make sure that you have new ways of handling stress, new ways of thinking about difficult relationship situations, and new ways of problem solving. When you leave this program, you should have lots of new tools to help you handle things differently. This will make it much less likely that the same problems will take place.

   Each session is designed to focus on a particular aspect of relationship health and/or relationship violence. Groups provide an atmosphere in which you can discuss the problems, feelings that have led to destructive behavior, and the impact violence has had on your relationship. New ways of understanding yourself, understanding others, and relating to other people are strongly emphasized.

5. *Is this a class or group counseling?*
   Although many of the group sessions may involve teaching of specific skills, such as stress management and improved communication, the groups are considered to be group counseling. This means that there is a strong emphasis placed on self-examination, discussion of feelings, and support for other group members. Most people benefit from the group based on how committed they are to engaging in these tasks.

6. *Do I have to come every week?*
   You are required to attend every week. Research indicates that there is a direct relationship between steady attendance and treatment progress. In order for you to benefit from the program, attendance must become a priority. As you become more involved in the group, you will probably find out that you are motivated to attend, not only for your own benefit but also for offering support to your fellow group members.

7. *What about absences?*
   We recognize that there may be circumstances that require you to miss a group session. If you are unable to attend a group session, please notify our staff beforehand to let us know that you will be

May not be reproduced without permission.

unable to attend. Documentation of all absences is required and should be given to our staff prior to your absence. If you miss a group for unexpected reasons, please bring in documentation for the absence at the next group session. Undocumented absences will be considered unexcused.

Unexcused absences indicate a lack of interest in or commitment to changing your situation. An unexcused absence will be grounds for a report back to your probation officer or other referring agency, which may result in the termination of treatment.

8. *What happens if I arrive late?*
If a group member arrives more than 5 minutes late, he will be marked as late. Three times late will be treated as the equivalent of one unexcused absence. If a group member arrives 15 or more minutes late, he will (under no circumstances) be allowed into the group, and this will be considered an unexcused absence.

9. *Who leads the groups?*
All of the group therapists are certified domestic violence counselors who have had extensive training in treatment of relationship violence.

10. *Are there additional expectations for successful participation other than group attendance?*
All sessions have homework assignments, which you will be expected to complete and bring to the next group meeting. The group leaders will review the homework assignment with you at the end of each group meeting so you will know what is expected. The group leaders will also discuss the completed homework at the beginning of each group meeting. Three missed homework assignments will be considered the equivalent of one unexcused absence. This will be grounds for a report back to your probation officer, case manager, social worker, or other referring agency, which may result in the termination of treatment.

Group members are required to be at the site 10 minutes before the time for the group to start in order to fill out the *Weekly Check-In* questionnaire. Group will not begin until everyone has completed the questionnaire.

You will be given a *STOP Program Handouts and Homework* binder at the first group meeting. Each week, information from the binder will be discussed during the group session. You are expected to bring your binder to each group meeting.

11. *What about confidentiality? Can what I say in the group be used against me?*
Because this treatment uses a team approach, you can assume that what you say in the group may be discussed with your probation officer, case manager, social worker, or other referring agency. Only information that is directly related to your treatment goals is included in these reports. Most of the personal issues and feelings discussed in the group sessions remain confidential.

In certain situations, the group leaders are obligated to report information that is revealed in the group. These reportable situations include serious threats of hurting or killing someone else, serious threats of hurting or killing yourself, new and significant reports of family violence (including incidents in which children have witnessed spousal abuse), child abuse, or elder abuse.

12. *What about new incidents of violence in my relationship?*
As a participant in domestic violence treatment you are expected to discuss any new incidents of violence in your relationships. Presenting such information does not necessarily lead to termination if you genuinely appear to be remorseful, take responsibility for your actions, and appear to be making efforts to prevent a similar reoccurrence in the future. Keep in mind that it is in your best interest to disclose a new incident of violence. When these incidents are discovered through other sources, it reflects on you negatively.

13. *What about electronic devices?*

During the group session, please turn off all electronic devices. You will have an opportunity at the break to reply to text or phone messages.

14. *How should I dress for the group?*

There is no specific dress code. However, clothing with inappropriate messages promoting or making light of sexism or violence or displaying otherwise inappropriate content will not be permitted.

15. *Any other rules about appropriate behavior?*

While you are in your group, you are asked to use respectful language that is not offensive to staff or other group members.

You may not use alcohol or drugs prior to the group session.

Group members will not threaten or intimidate the group or leaders at any time.

I have read the above information and agree to the conditions of treatment.

_____   _____

Group Member's Signature   Print Name

_____   _____

Date   Group Name

TYPICAL QUESTIONS AND CONCERNS

 **Handout**

1. *Won't group counseling try and get me to let out all my emotions? I'm not comfortable with that!*
   Everybody in group counseling is different, and each person decides how much of his personal emotions to reveal to others. No one is expected to walk right in and talk about their deepest feelings in front of a bunch of strangers.

   Over time, most people become more and more comfortable letting the group know more about what is happening inside. We know that there is usually a correlation between talking about yourself and getting some benefit from the sessions. But this all happens at the pace of the individual.

2. *I would rather have individual counseling because I don't like talking in front of other people and I can get more personal attention.*
   The STOP Program philosophy is that these kinds of problems are best treated in a group setting. You get the benefit of hearing about the experiences of others and learning from their successes and mistakes. The feedback from peers is one of the single most important factors in predicting positive outcome.

3. *I don't want to be in a group with a bunch of spouse abusers—I'm not like them!*
   We treat the man, not the label. We stay away from labels that sound like put-downs. Instead, we focus on the specific thoughts, feelings, and situations that have led to problem behaviors. We could put any man in this group, regardless of what has gone wrong in his behavior with others, and he would benefit from the approaches used in this treatment model.

May not be reproduced without permission.

PROVISIONAL STATUS POLICY (GROUP MEMBERS' VERSION)

 **Handout**

The following are grounds for group members to be placed on provisional status in the STOP Program (leading to possible termination). These behaviors are in addition to activity that takes place outside of the group sessions, such as acts of violence, repeated drug or alcohol problems, or failure to attend group:

1. **Consistent** put-downs of women or minimization of violence

2. **Persistent** disruptive or oppositional behavior in group

3. **Consistent** projection of blame for relationship problems without self-examination

4. **Consistent** lack of participation in group, including failure to complete homework assignments

5. **Consistent** pattern of "telling stories" (bragging or showing off) about controlling, abusive, or violent behavior with few or no signs of remorse

6. **Consistent** pattern of inappropriate messages on clothing (such as T-shirts with sexist messages)

May not be reproduced without permission.

THE 15 COMMANDMENTS OF STOP

 **Handout**

1. We are all 100% responsible for our own actions (even when it *feels* like someone else made us do it).

2. Violence is not an acceptable solution to problems.

3. Anger is normal. Being consumed by anger, or being driven to commit acts of aggression or retaliation because of anger, is not. It is your responsibility to recognize this and take action to stop it.

4. Recognize that anger is—always—a secondary emotion. Identify the primary one first and you are really in a position of power.

5. We do not have control over any other person, but we do have control over ourselves.

6. We can always take a Time-Out before reacting.

7. We can't do anything about the past, but we can change the future.

8. Self-talk is everything. We are always telling ourselves stories about the events in our world—and the stories can always change.

9. Sometimes anger can be very quiet and cold. Just because you are not yelling—or even if you are smiling—does not mean that you are not being aggressive.

10. Just because someone "deserves" retaliation doesn't mean that it is wise, productive, or moral to deliver it.

11. When you let go of anger, you are doing yourself a big favor. You are no longer allowing the situation or the person to control you.

12. Use gratitudes when you need to, and appreciate the power and positivity they will confer on you.

13. Always have a Prevention Plan in your back pocket. And think of the big picture.

14. Although there are differences between men and women, our needs and rights are fundamentally alike.

15. Counselors and case managers cannot make people change—they can only set the stage for change to occur.

May not be reproduced without permission.

GRATITUDE STATEMENTS

HUNTING THE GOOD STUFF!

 **Handout**

Research indicates that people who regularly acknowledge and express gratitudes are healthier, sleep better, and have better relationships. And they cope better with situations that might previously have made them angry or even violent.

At the beginning of each session, we will ask you to share some "good stuff" that you have "hunted" since we last met. For example:

■ *"I had a great conversation with my wife last night—I used what we learned in the group, and she said it was one of the best conversations we ever had. I am so grateful."*

■ *"I talked to a friend of mine and helped him out with a problem. I am grateful that I got a chance to do that."*

■ *"Somebody at work here really took one of my concerns seriously and followed through on it. I am really grateful."*

■ *"I watched my kids playing together last night and they were really getting along. I really felt lucky."*

May not be reproduced without permission.

FEELINGS COUNT

 **Handout**

HAPPY AND CONFIDENT

Accepted	Alive	Brave	Calm	Caring	Cheerful
Comfortable	Confident	Excited	Friendly	Fulfilled	Generous
Grateful	Happy	Hopeful	Joyful	Lovable	Loving
Peaceful	Playful	Powerful	Proud	Relaxed	Relieved
Respected	Secure	Understood	Valuable	Warm	Worthwhile

FEAR AND WORRY

Anxious	Apprehensive	Confused	Desperate	Distrustful
Fearful	Helpless	Horrified	Inhibited	Out-of-Control
Trapped	Panicky	Pressured	Threatened	Overwhelmed
Troubled	Uncertain	Uneasy	Uptight	Vulnerable
Worried				

ANGRY AND RESENTFUL

Angry	Bitter	Contemptuous	Disgusted	Disrespected
Frustrated	Furious	Hostile	Impatient	Irritated
Outraged	Provoked	Resentful	Stubborn	Unappreciated
Used	Victimized			

SAD AND PESSIMISTIC

Confused	Defeated	Depressed	Devastated	Disappointed
Discouraged	Helpless	Hopeless	Isolated	Lonely
Miserable	Trapped	Sad	Stuck	Overwhelmed
Useless				

UNCOMFORTABLE AND INSECURE

Awkward	Embarrassed	Foolish	Humiliated	Inhibited
Insecure	Self-conscious	Shy	Uncomfortable	

APOLOGETIC AND GUILTY

Apologetic	Guilty	Remorseful	Sorry	Untrustworthy

HURT AND REJECTED

Devastated	Excluded	Hurt	Ignored	Rejected	Vulnerable

JEALOUS AND LEFT OUT

Envious	Deprived	Left out	Jealous

ASHAMED AND INADEQUATE

Ashamed	Inferior	Inadequate	Incompetent	Stupid
Useless	Unattractive	Unworthy	Powerless	

May not be reproduced without permission.

PART III

NEW MEMBER SESSIONS

HOUSE OF ABUSE

THIS MATERIAL (OR THE MATERIAL FROM NEW MEMBER SESSION II) SHOULD BE PRESENTED ONLY WHEN AT LEAST ONE NEW GROUP MEMBER IS BEGINNING THE PROGRAM. THEN THE REGULARLY SCHEDULED GROUP CONTENT SHOULD RESUME.

NEW MEMBER SESSION I AND NEW MEMBER SESSION II SHOULD EACH BE PRESENTED ON ALTERNATE MONTHS.

Materials

House of Abuse

Program

1. In this New Member session, we recommend an exercise in which all group members are split up into dyads, interviewing each other *only* about basic information. This should take 10 minutes maximum. This is *not* the time to ask about or report information about the offense that led to their assignment to this program: *Please pair up with one of the group members next to you. You will have a few minutes each to get some basic information from your "partner": What is his name? Is he currently married or together with his partner? What is her name? Does he have kids? What are their names and ages? Where is he from? What kind of work does he do? What are his interests and hobbies? What does he expect to get out of this group? What does he think he can add to the group? You don't need to find out any details about how he ended up here in the group. We save that for much later. Then you will introduce your "partner" to the group.* At the end of this, and throughout the early group sessions, group leaders should seek out ways to establish connections among group members, such as those who are parents, those who are from similar parts of the country, and so on.

    Each partner then reports back to the group at large, "introducing" his partner to the rest of the group. Even if many of the men have already been through this exercise previously, they should still pair up with a new partner and go through it again.

Remember that, because of intermittent attendance, many of the group members may be new to each other even if this is not their own first session.

It is usually best to keep personal abuse and violence information to a minimum in the first session for a new group member.

2. Begin explaining the basic concept of the *House of Abuse* by drawing a diagram of the *House of Abuse* on the board. By the end of this program, the following categories will be listed in the different rooms:

- Physical Abuse
- Verbal/Emotional/Psychological
- Social Isolation
- Gender Privilege
- Intimidation
- Religion
- Sexual Abuse
- Child Abuse

3. It is also important to repeatedly emphasize the "100% rule." This rule states that we are each 100% responsible for our own behavior. Being angry or hurt does not have to lead to abuse or intimidation.

It has proven very valuable in this exercise to develop descriptions that are as gender-neutral as possible. Most of these forms of destructive conflicts can just as easily be used by a woman to a man as the other way around, with the obvious exceptions of, for the most part, sexual abuse. The goal here is to open up valuable discussion and to help the group members discuss these issues without feeling defensive.

4. Begin by asking for a definition of the most obvious kinds of destructive conflict, or abusive behavior, from one person in a relationship to another—this will usually involve physical abuse and probably yelling and screaming. Ask the question: *What are some ways that someone in an intimate adult relationship could be destructive or abusive to his or her partner? How can somebody abuse another?* As the group identifies different themes, label the different rooms, and fill in some of the examples in the room where they best fit. Here are some basic descriptions of what belongs in each room:

    a. **Physical Abuse.** This is the easiest to identify. This includes any kind of physical aggressive contact, including hitting, choking, and pushing. Make sure and review every possible form that the group can generate. The group members usually describe this first.

    b. **Verbal/Emotional/Psychological.** This is also easy to identify. This includes any kind of name calling, verbal put-downs, or criticism. This also involves the use of mind games. When a man "teases" a woman about her weight or body and then protests that he was only kidding or only asking a question, he is committing psychological abuse. When she humiliates him in public, she is doing the same thing. Often, men drill home the message that "you could never make it without me." When people hear this enough times, they may begin to believe it. Humiliating someone for not being successful or competent at something is psychological abuse. Another form of destructive conflict in this category is ignoring someone: the silent treatment. This can be one of the most powerful mind games of all, wearing someone down until he or she desperately tries to "be good."

c. **Intimidation.** This includes threats to kill or hurt the other person, threats against the kids, or threats of kidnapping the kids. It may involve telling her that a judge will never give her custody because she's crazy or she doesn't work or she has used drugs in the past. Threatening suicide is another example of intimidation—this can be a very powerful way of controlling someone because they are desperate to avoid the terrible guilt and pain. The goal of these gambits is to produce *fear*, which is used to maintain dominance and control.

d. **Sexual Abuse.** The most blatant form of sexual abuse is rape, which has only recently been declared a crime in a marriage. However, this is not the only form of sexual abuse in a relationship. Demanding that the partner watch or read pornography can be abusive. Insisting on certain sex acts that she finds humiliating or degrading can be abusive.

e. **Social Isolation.** This category is often overlooked. This is more typical male-to-female but could work the other way around. Because they feel threatened, men may become determined to prevent their wives or partners from becoming independent or successful. This may involve sabotaging the woman's attempts to work, go to school, or have friends or activities of her own. The fear for a man here is that the woman won't need him anymore if she develops in this way. This is the ultimate indication of insecurity—the man has to keep her down so that he can feel more confident and dominant.

f. **Gender Privilege**. The male gender privilege form of destructive conflicts includes the entitlement men claim that leads them to dominate the relationship. The man who insists on using the fact that he is the breadwinner to demand that he make decisions for the marriage and family would be an example. This same attitude can be used to demand sex, get out of household chores, or demand more control over his free time than his wife or partner is allowed. A man may tell his wife or partner that he "needs" to go away with his buddies for a week; what would it be like if she told him the same thing and if she just assumed that he would watch the kids and take care of the business at home?

The female gender privilege form of destructive conflicts includes the female's insistence that she have more control over child-rearing decisions or the color of the new sofa. If a woman insists that she shouldn't have to work because *that's the man's job*, we have an example of female gender privilege.

g. **Religion.** Using religion as a form of abuse involves invoking the Bible as a rationalization for domination. It should be pointed out that, like statistics, the Bible can be interpreted as an explanation for just about anything. Be careful here—making remarks that might seem disrespectful about the Bible or religion can be very damaging to initial rapport. It is often helpful to start out by suggesting that one form of destructive conflict can be restricting a partner's right to go to the church he or she wants, or insisting that he participate in religion when he doesn't want to. As the discussion moves on, try asking the question, "How could someone use the Bible as a form of destructive conflict?"

h. **Child Abuse.** Any physical, sexual, verbal, or emotional form of child abuse is likewise a destructive conflict to the marriage. Using the kids as pawns in the battle between parents or threatening to hurt the kids would be examples here also. This can often lead to a discussion about the ways in which abused children often become abusers themselves in the next generation.

After establishing the rooms of the House of Abuse, ask the group members to consider the following questions:

- *Is this a house that you would like to live in?*
- *You don't have to say anything out loud, but see if you recognize any of these rooms as rooms in your house right now.*
- *Again, don't say anything out loud, but see if your recognize any of these rooms as rooms in the house you grew up in.*
- *Would you say that most of the examples we have come up with are illegal or criminal behavior? If not, then be aware that we are defining abusive behavior in relationships as anything that is clearly hurtful or destructive in this relationship—even if you can't go to jail for it.*

NEW MEMBER SESSION I

THE HOUSE OF ABUSE

 **Handout**

Physical Abuse	Intimidation	Child Abuse
Verbal/Emotional/Psychological		Social Isolation
Religion	Gender Privilege	Sexual Abuse

*The House of Abuse chart was developed by Michael F. McGrane, MSW, LICSW, Director of the Violence Prevention & Intervention Services (VPIS) of the Amherst H. Wilder Foundation, and is used here by permission. The chart is part of a complete domestic abuse curriculum entitled *Foundations for Violence-Free Living: A Step-by-Step Guide to Facilitating Men's Domestic Abuse Groups*, available from Fieldstone Alliance at 1-800-274-6024. May not be reproduced without permission.

TIME-OUT

Materials

Time-Out
Time-Out Information for Partners
When Your Partner Blocks Your Path

Program

1. In this New Member session, we recommend an exercise in which all group members are split up into dyads, interviewing each other *only* about basic information. This should take 10 minutes maximum. This is *not* the time to ask about or report information about the offense that led to their assignment to this program: *Please pair up with one of the group members next to you. You will have a few minutes each to get some basic information from your "partner": What is his name? Is he currently married or together with his partner? What is her name? Does he have kids? What are their names and ages? Where is he from? What kind of work does he do? What are his interests and hobbies? What do you expect to get out of this group? What do you think you can add to the group? You don't need to find out any details about how they ended up here in the group. We save that for much later. Then you will introduce your "partner" to the group.* At the end of this, and throughout the early group sessions, group leaders should seek out ways to establish connections among group members, such as those who are parents or those who are from similar parts of the country.

   Each partner then reports back to the group at large, "introducing" his partner to the rest of the group. Even if many of the men have already been through this exercise previously, they should still pair up with a new partner and go through it again.

   Remember that, because of intermittent attendance, many of the group members may be new to each other even if this is not their own first session.

   It is usually best to keep personal abuse and violence information to a minimum in the first session for a new group member.

2. TIME-OUT
   a. Introduce the idea of having a plan for episodes when it feels like behavior is getting out of control. This requires personal responsibility—to recognize the

signals and to act responsibly in those situations. The odds of being successful with this plan are much higher when people have thought about it, planned for it, and rehearsed it in advance.

b. Review the *Time-Out* technique: The technique does not help the couple resolve the issue at hand; thus, it is a "stopgap" measure. However, it often prevents violence, which is the primary goal. Communication skills can be learned later, after the fear of any destructive behavior (verbal or physical abuse) is gone.

Model the use of the skill with a co-leader or one of the group members.

Make sure that the group members inform their partners—*in advance*—of the purpose and steps involved with the *Time-Out.*

c. Review the *Time-Out Information for Partners* handout. Be prepared for the group discussion in which the group members protest that their partners will never put up with a *Time-Out.* It is important to empathize with this concern because, in many cases, it is legitimate. Emphasize that we are offering approaches that are not guaranteed to work but that simply decrease the probability of an explosion.

d. Review *When Your Partner Blocks Your Path.* One of the group members (or group leaders) should stand near the doorway, blocking a group member's path out of the room. Explain to the person trying to leave that it is his job, if he is ever blocked from being able to exit by his partner in an explosive situation, to find a way out without "putting hands on." This is a very controversial subject. The group members (particularly men who have been charged with domestic violence) will often loudly complain—in some cases, rightfully so—that they don't have any good options in this situation. Our job here is to empathize with the difficulty of being in this position while strategizing the least dangerous and destructive ways to get out of it. It is essential to remind the group members that all of these strategies contain significant risks, but that the alternative—violence between intimate partners—is worse.

NEW MEMBER SESSION II

TIME-OUT

 **Handout**

The Time-Out is an emergency strategy to prevent the dangerous escalation of conflicts. It should *only* be used in a crisis—and as you learn better communication and self-management skills, it may never have to be used at all. But you must know how to use it effectively.

> **IF YOU USE A TIME-OUT FREQUENTLY, SOMETHING IS SERIOUSLY WRONG WITH YOUR RELATIONSHIP. DO NOT USE A TIME-OUT SIMPLY BECAUSE YOU WISH TO AVOID TALKING ABOUT A CERTAIN SUBJECT. THIS IS FOR EMERGENCIES ONLY, AND YOU MUST BE PREPARED TO RESUME THE DISCUSSION LATER ON.**

The Time-Out should not be used as a weapon against the other person. It should not be used as a way of avoiding conflicts. It should not be used as a way of making the other person feel abandoned (*"I'm outta here, babe—I'll show you who's in charge!"*).

Instead, the Time-Out should be used as a sign of respect for the relationship. The message is this: *I care enough about us that I don't want any more damage to this relationship.*

It is essential that your partner understand this message of respect. It is your job to clearly explain this in advance and to follow it up by your actions when using the Time-Out correctly.

1. *I'm beginning to feel like things are getting out of control.*

2. *And I don't want to do anything that would mess up our relationship.*

3. *So I need to take a Time-Out.*

4. *I'm going out for a walk around the neighborhood (or my sister's house, or the gym, etc.).*

5. *I'll be back in (5 minutes, or 1 hour, etc.)*

6. *And let's try talking about this again when I get back. Okay?*

The partner responds:

7. *Okay. Time-Out.*

If he or she does not acknowledge, begin the Time-Out anyway—*without* making any physical contact or threats!

> Leave silently—no door slamming.
> While away, don't drink or use drugs—and don't drive if your temper is out of control.
> Try using "self-talk" that will help you keep this in perspective:
>
> - *I'm getting upset, but I don't have to lose my cool!*
> - *I'm frustrated, but I don't have to control anybody else or always get my way.*
> - *I can calm myself and think through this situation.*
> - *I've got to think about what will be most important for the future.*

May not be reproduced without permission.

Do something physical (walking, playing sports, working out, etc.) if it will help you discharge tension. Try distracting yourself with any activity that temporarily takes your mind off the intensity of the argument.

You must come back when you said you would; otherwise, you need to call and check in. When you come back, decide together if you want to continue the discussion. Here are the options at this point:

- **Discuss it now:** This is usually the best and most respectful action, but there are some exceptions.

- **Drop the issue:** Maybe you both realize now that it was really not that big a deal.

- **Put the issue on hold:** This may be important to discuss, but it would be better to do it at a later time. As long as *both* parties agree, this can work.

Each person has the right to say "no" to further discussion at that time and to suggest a time for discussion. If anger escalates again, take another Time-Out.

TIME-OUT INFORMATION FOR PARTNERS*

 **Handout**

Please note that this form is written as if males are taking the Time-Outs and females have questions about what to do. **These same instructions can, and should apply, in any combination of partner violence, including male-to-female, female-to-male, straight or gay.** Please change the pronouns to fit your personal situation, if appropriate.

1. **How do Time-Outs help solve our family problems?**
   Your partner's use of Time-Outs will prevent him from escalating into physical or psychological abuse. Time-Outs alone do not solve destructive conflicts, but if used faithfully they will help him avoid extremely destructive behavior. Family problems have to be discussed and solutions agreed upon. This cannot happen if one person is abusive of the other. No communication takes place when there is abuse. Time-Outs are a necessary first step to communicating respectfully.

2. **What do I do if every time I want to discuss an important topic with my partner, he says he is taking a Time-Out?**
   Let him take the Time-Out anyway. If he becomes angry and abusive, you will not be able to talk about the problems. At first he may take Time-Outs a lot. Just remind yourself that it is only one step and that he will be expected to use other approaches as well. Read the instruction sheet—it will help you understand how it works.

3. **What if he refuses to discuss the matter even after the Time-Out?**
   Notice on the instruction sheet that he has several choices as to what he does after a Time-Out. He is not supposed to drop issues if they are important to you. However, he may put them on hold until he is able to both calmly speak and *listen to you*. If he refuses to discuss an issue, your insisting will *not* bring about the communication. Let him know that you are still interested in talking about the issue, but be willing to set a later time when he can be calmer when discussing it.

4. **Should I remind my partner to take a Time-Out when he is getting angry or abusive?**
   No. He is responsible for identifying his own feelings and taking the Time-Out. As long as you do it for him, he is *not* doing his job. If you are upset about his abuse, you take a Time-Out for yourself as long as you can do it safely. Remember: You cannot control another person's behavior; you can only protect yourself.

5. **What should I do when he takes a Time-Out during a discussion?**
   Remind yourself that this is the first step—that it is better for him to take a Time-Out than to be abusive toward you. Waiting for him to return can lead to your feeling frustrated or abandoned. You can use the time in a Time-Out for yourself and then go about your regular business.

---

*Adapted with permission from the Family Violence Prevention Fund's publication entitled *Domestic Violence: A National Curriculum for Family Preservation Practitioners*, written by Susan Schecter, MSW, and Anne L. Ganley, PhD. May not be reproduced without permission.

6. **Would Time-Outs be useful for me?**

   Yes, if you find your own anger rising, a Time-Out is a tool you can use to calm down before you go further in working out a conflict. However, your using Time-Outs for yourself will not necessarily change your partner's behaviors. Time-Outs are good for you to use when you are in conflicts with your children or with other people.

WHEN YOUR PARTNER BLOCKS YOUR PATH

 **Handout**

Sometimes, your partner will not cooperate with your attempts to take a Time-Out, no matter how respectful you are. Here is a sequence that sometimes will occur:

1. You declare a Time-Out (following the steps correctly).

2. Your partner blocks your path so you cannot leave.

3. Now you should remind her of the Time-Out agreement that you have previously discussed.

4. But she continues to block your path.

5. Offer *your partner* the opportunity to leave instead of you, so she does not feel abandoned by you. For example, you might say, "OK, if you want to leave, that's cool too. I don't want you to feel like I'm leaving you. We just need a break right now until things calm down."

In this situation, you cannot afford to place any hands on your partner or to use any significant force to move her. Not only is this dangerous and disrespectful, but it is very likely that YOU will be arrested.

If none of these are successful in separating the two of you, you have three basic options:

I. Physical Escape

- Retreat through another exit (into a bathroom or a bedroom) and lock the door.
- Escape through a window if it is safe to do so.
- Agree to stay and discuss the situation until your partner relaxes and no longer blocks the door, then escape.

II. Calling for Help

- Dial 911. Explain that your partner will not allow you to leave the premises. Make it clear that you are trying to avoid violence.
- Call someone who can talk to your partner and try to calm her down to cooperate with the Time-Out.
- Scream for help.

III. Staying Put

- Sit down and stay quiet. Repeat self-talk to yourself such as "It's not worth it to get into a fight" or "It's my job to stay calm now." Use relaxation techniques, like deep breathing, to help you stay calm.

None of these options are particularly great. They all contain significant risks, but they are designed to accomplish the most important goal in this situation: preventing both of you from getting hurt. We hope that you are never in this situation, but these are important strategies to keep in mind just in case.

May not be reproduced without permission.

PART IV

EXIT/RELAPSE PREVENTION SESSIONS

EXIT SESSION I

MOST VIOLENT AND/OR MOST DISTURBING INCIDENT

 **Handout**

**THIS MATERIAL (AND THE MATERIAL FROM EXIT SESSION II)
SHOULD BE PRESENTED ONLY WHEN AT LEAST ONE GROUP MEMBER
IS NEAR THE END POINT OF THE TREATMENT PROGRAM.
THEN THE REGULARLY SCHEDULED GROUP CONTENT SHOULD RESUME.**

Program

1. Here are the suggested instructions for this very important exercise for a group member who is close to terminating the group program:

Tell us, in detail, the most disturbing abusive incident in your relationship <u>that you have committed</u>. This is not necessarily the most physically injurious event or the one you got busted for, but rather the one that stands out as the most emotionally upsetting.

There may have been other more abusive incidents in your relationship committed by your partner— but this assignment is to choose a situation when YOU have behaved the most abusively toward her.

It is very important for you to describe this incident as vividly as possible, in detail, as if it were happening in slow motion. Each step of the way, we need to hear about your self-talk, your emotions, and your physical state.

(Note to the group leader: Particularly important is his affect. You may need to say repeatedly, "Describe how you are feeling at this point." The goal here is to diminish as much of the original denial and minimization as possible.)

We think you're ready for this now in ways that you were not when you first came in to this program. This is an opportunity to go into more depth with these issues—particularly with some of the new skills and information that you now have.

We also want you to identify your partner's and child's self-talk, your partner's and child's emotions, and your partner's and child's physical states.

We know you can do this.

May not be reproduced without permission.

PREVENTION PLAN

THIS MATERIAL (AND THE MATERIAL FROM EXIT SESSION I) SHOULD BE PRESENTED ONLY WHEN AT LEAST ONE GROUP MEMBER IS AT APPROXIMATELY THE END POINT OF THE TREATMENT PROGRAM. THEN THE REGULARLY SCHEDULED GROUP CONTENT SHOULD RESUME.

Materials

Prevention Plan

Program

1. Explain that the *Prevention Plan* is based on a treatment called "cue therapy," which was originally developed to treat cocaine abusers at a veterans' center. Clinical research showed that, even though the patients were exposed to many excellent treatments, many relapsed because they could not resist the old familiar "cues" that triggered the familiar drug pattern. Cue Therapy was introduced so that they could carefully rehearse exposure to these cues while practicing many alternative coping strategies.

2. Ask the terminating group member to identify a cue or trigger for his own aggression. Then guide him through each of the different coping strategies. At the completion, he should have generated one strategy from each category.

3. Now role-play the cue situation and ask the volunteer to practice each of the coping strategies. Explain that, in real situations, it is rarely practical to use all of these. However, it is valuable to be equipped with as many as possible just in case.

4. *Challenges:* Who should you *not* talk to? (thanks to James Reavis, PsyD, for developing this technique): Discuss how important peer groups are in maintaining new attitudes and behaviors. Ask the group to role-play "negative" influences on the terminating group member.

   For example, ask the group member to role-play the following situation:

It's Friday after work, and you're playing basketball with some friends. The game is winding down and your friends invite you out for some beers with them.

You remember that your wife planned to make dinner for the two of you tonight and she asked you to be home by 6:30. You tell the guys that you have to pass, because of these plans.

Group members should challenge him by saying some of the following:

- *You used to be so much fun—what's happened to you, man?*
- *You can't let her get away with that crap!*
- *Prove to her who's in charge!*
- *Just lie to her, man—you know how they all are!*

The selected group member should practice his response to this.

In generating the *Prevention Plan*, there are three principles to keep in mind:

1. Be very specific about problem behavior:

GENERAL	SPECIFIC (Much better)
Losing my temper	*Pushing my son*
Blowing it	*Yelling at my co-worker*

2. Be very specific about trigger behavior:

GENERAL	SPECIFIC (Much better)
Feeling disrespected	*When my wife puts me down for not making enough money*

3. Use input from the group members—they are experts at this!

EXIT SESSION II

PREVENTION PLAN*

 **Handout**

Purpose: To prepare you for future situations when you might be tempted to become abusive with your partner.

Cue or Trigger (What could set you off?):

Coping Strategies:

1. **SCARE YOURSELF IMAGE—Example:** Remember the damage to your family, remember being arrested, etc. What scary image would have an impact on you?

2. **SELF-TALK—Example:** "This isn't worth it," "Nobody's perfect," "I want to keep my life together." What would that be for you?

3. **RELAXATION/DISTRACTION—Example:** Deep breathing, listening to music, playing basketball, etc. What would work for you?

4. **FRIENDS/ALLIES—Example:** Call a friend, crisis line, therapist, sponsor, or family member. Who would that be for you?

Behavior I Do NOT Want To Do (be specific):

_____

_____

*Adapted with permission from Wexler (1991). May not be reproduced without permission.

PART V
CORE
CURRICULUM

Session 1

THE RED FLAGS OF ANGER

Materials

> The Cycle of Abuse
> Red Flags Exercise
> The Four-Square Technique

Program

1. Ask each group member to report one "gratitude."

2. Focus on the "mindfulness" exercise for 1 minute.

3. Review the homework from the previous week.

4. Review the *Weekly Check-Ins* and use these to help guide the group discussion in the first half of the group.

5. Present the *Cycle of Abuse* handout. The handout focuses on the three primary stages in the cycle of family violence: (1) tension building (escalation); (2) violence (explosion); and (3) calm loving (honeymoon). Explain to the men that this cycle is an accurate description of the patterns in *some* couples where abuse takes place. It is particularly helpful when working with women who have been abused, because it helps them see the patterns of behavior more clearly. However, not all couples follow this pattern. It is not inevitable that abusive behavior escalates in frequency and intensity, as the original model suggested. And not all men perceive this pattern as being the most accurate description of their own behavior. It is better to address these issues up front to defuse resistance to this model.

   a. First, present an overview of the three stages and ask the group members if they recognize some of the signs from each stage.

   b. Next, discuss the tension-building stage. What are the cues and triggers that are likely to provoke the escalation? You will be reviewing the *red flags* that trigger this escalation in the next discussion.

   c. Discuss the honeymoon phase. Here, the tables often turn, and the person who has been so domineering becomes very dependent. The abusive person recognizes how much he or needs the partner and may often cling desperately. This stage can be extremely difficult for the partner to resist, because the vulnerable emotions are so appealing. In keeping with the basic principles of behavioral psychology, both partners may feel "reinforced" for the explosion. They may come to believe (unconsciously) that **this state can only be achieved in the aftermath of violence.**

6. Introduce the concept of *red flags*. Go over the *Red Flags of Anger* exercise. Explain how important it is to identify the warning signs of anger. Remind the group members that the more they know about themselves, the more "true power" they have over their own behavior.

    PHYSICAL *red flags*: muscle tension, heartbeat, disorientation, etc. (*What are the indicators in your body that let you know you are starting to climb the escalation ladder?*)

    SITUATIONAL *red flags*: paying bills, hearing certain questions, dealing with kids, after having a few drinks, etc. (*What are the situations that are almost sure to start an argument between you and other people? When you know what these are, you can plan a whole lot better—either by avoiding some of them, or by being extra careful to monitor your own behavior*)

    SELF-TALK *red flags*: (Discuss Dutton's "bitch tape" [1998]. Dutton's research found that abusive men identified self-talk like "What a bitch!" or "I can't believe I have to put up with such a bitch!" as narrative triggers for abusive behavior. Ask the group members to identify their own "bitch tapes.")

    "*He's trying to make a fool of me.*"
    "*She doesn't love me anymore.*"
    "*I think she wants to leave me.*"
    "*That asshole thinks he's better than I am.*"
    "*Somebody needs to teach her a lesson!*"

7. Ask each group member to role-play a personal situation including all of the above types of *red flags*: physical, situational, self-talk. Make sure the other group members are genuinely convinced that they can "see" the *red flags*.

8. Review *The Four-Square Technique* and discuss.

THE CYCLE OF ABUSE*

Domestic abuse typically follows a pattern consisting of three phases that are repeated, with some variations over and over.

The first phase is the tension-building phase: a time when the abuser is becoming more irritable, moody, and impatient and the partner is "walking on eggshells" trying to prevent an increase or outburst of abusive behavior.

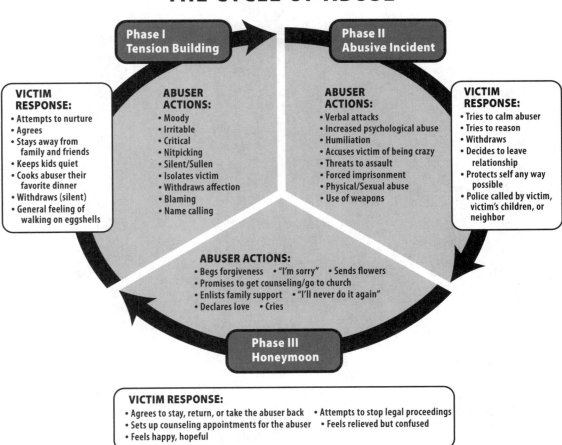

THE CYCLE OF ABUSE

Phase I
Tension Building

Phase II
Abusive Incident

VICTIM RESPONSE:
• Attempts to nurture
• Agrees
• Stays away from family and friends
• Keeps kids quiet
• Cooks abuser their favorite dinner
• Withdraws (silent)
• General feeling of walking on eggshells

ABUSER ACTIONS:
• Moody
• Irritable
• Critical
• Nitpicking
• Silent/Sullen
• Isolates victim
• Withdraws affection
• Blaming
• Name calling

ABUSER ACTIONS:
• Verbal attacks
• Increased psychological abuse
• Humiliation
• Accuses victim of being crazy
• Threats to assault
• Forced imprisonment
• Physical/Sexual abuse
• Use of weapons

VICTIM RESPONSE:
• Tries to calm abuser
• Tries to reason
• Withdraws
• Decides to leave relationship
• Protects self any way possible
• Police called by victim, victim's children, or neighbor

ABUSER ACTIONS:
• Begs forgiveness   • "I'm sorry"   • Sends flowers
• Promises to get counseling/go to church
• Enlists family support   • "I'll never do it again"
• Declares love   • Cries

Phase III
Honeymoon

VICTIM RESPONSE:
• Agrees to stay, return, or take the abuser back   • Attempts to stop legal proceedings
• Sets up counseling appointments for the abuser   • Feels relieved but confused
• Feels happy, hopeful

---

*Originally published as the Cycle of Violence in *The Battered Woman*, by Lenore Walker (1980). May not be reproduced without permission.

Phase two is the "acute battering" or "abusive phase." The abusive phase is characterized by an increase in the severity of abuse that may or may not include physical or sexual violence. During an acute phase a victim may flee, seek medical attention, or tell someone about the abuse.

The third phase is usually called the "honeymoon" phase. It is characterized by relative calm, apologies, and promises by the abuser to change. The victim may feel both relief and confusion. The victim often believes the abuser, not recognizing that the "honeymoon" phase is also intended to control the victim and keep the victim in the relationship.

RED FLAGS EXERCISE

 **Handout**

Red flags are warnings. They tell us that we are entering an emotional state, a way of thinking, or a situation where we may feel really angry, lose control, and/or escalate. Becoming aware of these red flags helps us remain in control of our selves and behaviors.

Physical Red Flag Cues

What physical cues (cues in your body) will tell you that you are getting really angry and beginning to escalate?

Red Flag Self-Talk

What kind of self-talk do you begin to have when your anger is rising and you are beginning to escalate?

Red Flag Situations

What kinds of situations usually result in conflicts, where your anger rises and you begin to escalate?

May not be reproduced without permission.

THE FOUR-SQUARE TECHNIQUE

 **Handout**

The *Four-Square Technique* is especially valuable when you are trying to decide how to act. It might be something of major consequence, like whether to be violent with someone, or more of an everyday experience, like how to express your disappointment or unhappiness with one of your kids.

Every decision you make involves four outcomes to consider:

SHORT TERM/SELF	LONG TERM/SELF
SHORT TERM/OTHER	LONG TERM/OTHER

For example, if you are tempted to get drunk at a party (but your wife often suffers when you do this), your *Four-Square* might look like this:

SHORT TERM/SELF **Great!**	LONG TERM/SELF **Guilty**
SHORT TERM/OTHER **Hurtful**	LONG TERM/OTHER **Angry/Mistrusting**

Practically everything that you are tempted to do, like getting angry or aggressive, means that the "Short Term/Self" square is very appealing—otherwise you wouldn't be so tempted to do it. But, before you act, it is very important to consider the other three squares. *Will this be a good decision for other people? Will this be a good decision for me in the long run?*

If the vote on the *Four-Square* is 3 to 1 against, or even 2 to 2, it is usually a good idea to not go there.

May not be reproduced without permission.

HOMEWORK

Handout

1. Pick out a situation where you were tempted to get angry or show an attitude with someone. Fill out the boxes in the *Four-Square* and be prepared to discuss this in the next session.

2. Fill out the *Anger Styles Quiz* in preparation for the next session.

May not be reproduced without permission.

Session 2
ANGER STYLES

Materials

Anger Styles Quiz
Anger Styles
Letting Go of Anger

Program

1. Ask each group member to report one "gratitude."

2. Focus on the "mindfulness" exercise for 1 minute.

3. Review the homework from the previous week.

4. Review the *Weekly Check-Ins* and use these to help guide the group discussion in the first half of the group.

5. Review *Anger Styles* and the *Anger Styles Quiz*. Use the group members' answers from the *Anger Styles Quiz* to help generate a discussion about the different styles of anger that they use.

6. Review *Letting Go of Anger*.

ANGER STYLES QUIZ*

Handout

1. I try never to get angry.   Yes   No
2. I get really nervous when others are angry.   Yes   No
3. I feel I'm doing something bad when I get angry.   Yes   No
4. I tell people I'll do what they want, but then I often forget.   Yes   No
5. I say things like "Yeah, but. . . " and "I'll do it later."   Yes   No
6. People tell me I must be angry but I'm not sure why.   Yes   No
7. I get jealous a lot, even when there is no reason.   Yes   No
8. I don't trust people very much.   Yes   No
9. Sometimes it feels like people are out to get me.   Yes   No
10. My anger comes on really fast.   Yes   No
11. I act before I think when I get angry.   Yes   No
12. My anger goes away very quickly after I explode.   Yes   No
13. I get very angry when people criticize me.   Yes   No
14. People say I am easily hurt and oversensitive.   Yes   No
15. I get angry when I feel bad about myself.   Yes   No
16. I get mad in order to get what I want.   Yes   No
17. I try to scare others with my anger.   Yes   No
18. I can pretend to be very mad when I'm really okay.   Yes   No
19. Sometimes I get angry just for the excitement or action.   Yes   No
20. I like the strong feelings that come with my anger.   Yes   No
21. My anger takes over and I go out of control.   Yes   No
22. I seem to get angry all the time.   Yes   No
23. I just can't break the habit of getting angry a lot.   Yes   No
24. I get mad without thinking—it just happens.   Yes   No
25. I become very angry when I defend my beliefs and opinions.   Yes   No
26. I feel outraged about what others try to get away with.   Yes   No
27. I always know I'm right in an argument.   Yes   No
28. I hang on to my anger for a long time.   Yes   No
29. I have a hard time forgiving people.   Yes   No
30. I hate people for what they've done to me.   Yes   No

*Reprinted with permission by New Harbinger Publications, Inc., from Potter-Efron & Potter-Efron (1995), www.newharbinger.com. May not be reproduced without permission.

ANGER STYLES*

 **Handout**

Anger is an important emotion that tells you something is wrong. It pushes you into action. It's a messenger that you must not ignore. But anger can cause problems, especially when you get stuck in it. The styles listed below are based on the *Anger Styles Quiz* that you filled out.

Masked Anger Styles (Items 1–9)

The hidden, or masked, anger styles are hardest to recognize as anger.

Anger avoiders fear and deny their anger. They simply don't want to own their anger. When they see that messenger coming, they head the other way. Anger avoiders need to admit that everybody gets angry once in a while. They need to accept their own anger as part of themselves.

Anger sneakers let their anger come out sideways, through such actions as forgetting their promises and acting helpless. Anger sneakers frustrate others with their inactivity. Their anger sneaks out in the many clever ways they find not to do things. Anger sneakers most need to learn how to be direct with their anger.

Paranoid anger is another form of masked anger. People who feel paranoid give away their anger. They are convinced others are furious with them, when they are really the ones who are irate. Paranoids must take back their own anger and learn to be careful with it, before they can get better.

Explosive Anger Styles (Items 10–18)

The explosive anger styles are dangerous, powerful, and alarming. People with these styles become very angry and lose control.

One kind of explosive anger is sudden anger. Sudden anger strikes like a tornado in the night. People with sudden anger must learn to recognize cues that their anger is building and to slow down the process.

Shame-based anger is an explosive style that comes with a person's low self-esteem. The worse people feel about themselves, the more likely they are to be oversensitive to criticism and to think others are trying to belittle them. The antidote for shame-based anger is improved self-worth.

Deliberate anger is intentional. People use deliberate anger to get their way by scaring others. It's a crude technique that often backfires, but it's also hard to give up because it does work some of the time. People with deliberate anger need to learn new and better ways to ask for what they want.

The last explosive style is addictive anger. Anger addicts seek out the intense feelings that come with rage. Their anger helps them feel alive and powerful. Anger addicts need to treat their anger as an addiction by making a commitment to decline all anger binges and by learning how to live life in moderation.

---

*Reprinted with permission by New Harbinger Publications, Inc., from Potter-Efron & Potter-Efron (1995), www .newharbinger.com. May not be reproduced without permission.

Chronic Anger Styles (Items 19–30)

Chronic anger styles endure for long periods, even years. They trap people in endless bouts of anger, gluing them to their anger like a fly to flypaper.

One kind of long-term anger is habitual anger. People with this type of anger don't even think about why they are angry. They just are. Habitually angry people need to break the habit by becoming more aware of their actions and substituting new behavior and thoughts.

Moral anger, another type of chronic anger, comes to people who defend their anger by convincing themselves they are right and good while their opponents are both wrong and bad. To escape this prison people must let go of their feeling of superiority. They must learn to treat others as equals even when they disagree.

Haters store up resentments and treat themselves as helpless victims. Self-haters despise themselves for what they see as their weaknesses. Both live in the past and cannot enjoy life. They need to learn how to forgive themselves as helpless victims.

Each anger style poses a challenge if your goal is to handle anger well. That's why it is important to understand your personal anger style or styles. The more you know about your patterns of thinking and acting, the more control you will have over your life. You can indeed learn to let go of excessive anger and resentment.

LETTING GO OF ANGER*

 **Handout**

Anger is a part of life. Our wish for you, and for ourselves, is to be able to accept the blessing of anger, to listen to its message, and then let go of it.

DO'S AND DON'TS FOR TREATING OTHERS WITH RESPECT

Do . . .

  begin each day with a promise to respect others
  sit down and talk quietly
  listen carefully to what others say
  look for things to appreciate in others
  give praise out loud for the good you see in others
  tell others they are good, good enough, and lovable
  tell others they are worthwhile and important to you
  speak in a quiet voice even when you disagree
  pass up chances to insult, attack, or criticize
  let others have responsibility for their lives while you take responsibility for yours

Don't . . .

  look for things to criticize
  make fun or laugh at others
  make faces or roll your eyes
  tell others how to run their lives
  insult others
  ignore others
  put people down in front of others
  act superior
  sneer
  tell others they're weird or crazy
  say others are bad, not good enough, or unlovable
  say others don't belong or you wish they were dead
  call others names like fat, ugly, stupid, or worthless

---

*Adapted from Potter-Efron & Potter-Efron (1995). May not be reproduced without permission.

HOMEWORK

 **Handout**

Record three examples of your anger that fit into the category of your anger style. These examples can be from this week or from the past.

1.

2.

3.

May not be reproduced without permission.

Session 3
TRAUMA AND ANGER

Materials

Red Flags of Trauma
Trauma: Response and Recovery
The Stories of Trauma

Program

1. Ask each group member to report one "gratitude."

2. Focus on the "mindfulness" exercise for 1 minute.

3. Review the homework from the previous week.

4. Review the *Weekly Check-Ins* and use these to help guide the group discussion in the first half of the group.

5. Review and discuss *Red Flags of Trauma*. Explain that previous experiences of trauma (military, childhood abuse, witnessing violence, etc.) can often make someone more likely to have a wide range of emotional and behavioral reactions—including violence. The purpose of this discussion is, as always, to help group members become more truly powerful over their lives by knowing themselves better.

   Reviewing trauma history can never be used to excuse violent behavior—but self-knowledge makes group members even more truly responsible for their own behavior.

6. Review and discuss *Trauma: Response and Recovery*.

7. Review and discuss *The Stories of Trauma*.

RED FLAGS OF TRAUMA*

Handout

1. RE-EXPERIENCING THE EVENT

Nightmares about the event or other scary dreams

Flashbacks, when you act or feel as if the incident is recurring

Intrusive memories that suddenly pop into your mind—you might have these when there is something to remind you of the event (including anniversaries of the event) or even when there is nothing there to remind you of it

Common times to have these memories are when you are falling asleep, when you relax, or when you are bored. These symptoms are all normal following such a traumatic event. You are NOT going crazy.

2. EMOTIONAL AROUSAL

When reminded of the event, you may experience intense emotions/physical reactions:

Problems falling or staying asleep

Irritability or outbursts of anger

Difficulty concentrating

Startle reactions, like jumping at noises or when someone walks up behind you

Being "on guard"/looking over your shoulder even when there is no reason to

3. AVOIDANCE

A natural reaction to intrusive memories and strong emotional reactions is the urge to push these thoughts and feelings away:

Avoid places or people who remind you of the event

Avoid watching certain television programs or turn off the TV

Avoid reading the newspaper or watching the news

Avoid thinking about the event or letting yourself feel your feelings about the event

Avoid certain sights, sounds, or smells that remind you of the event

Difficulty remembering all or part of the event

Feeling numb and cut-off from the world around you—this feeling of detachment or numbness is another form of avoidance; sometimes it is described as feeling as though you are watching life from behind glass

*Adapted from Resick, P. A., Monson, C. M., & Chard, K. M. (2007). *Cognitive processing therapy: Veteran/Military version.* Washington, DC: Department of Veterans Affairs. May not be reproduced without permission.

TRAUMA: RESPONSE AND RECOVERY*

 **Handout**

In the time immediately following a trauma, most people will have stress symptoms. However, for many people, those symptoms naturally decrease, and they usually recover from the traumatic event.

There are some people who do not recover without help. Based on that, it is helpful to think of post-traumatic stress disorder (PTSD) as a problem in recovery. Something gets in the way of that natural process of recovery. We need to determine what got in the way and to change it so that you can recover from what happened—AND ESPECIALLY SO THAT YOUR REACTION TO TRAUMA DOES NOT LEAD YOU TO HURT THE PEOPLE YOU LOVE.

1. When people face serious, possibly life-threatening events, they experience a strong physical reaction called the *fight or flight* response—or a third possibility, the *freeze* response. Your body is trying to get you ready to fight or flee danger. The goal is to get all the blood and oxygen out to your hands, feet, and big muscle groups so that you can run or fight.

   You might feel like you have been kicked in the gut or are going to faint. Your body stops fighting off diseases and digesting food. You're not thinking about your life philosophy and you may have trouble "thinking" at all!

   The same thing happens with the freeze response, but here your body is trying to reduce distress. You may have stopped feeling distress or had the sense that this was happening to someone else as if it were a movie. You might have shut down emotionally or even felt like you were out of your body or that time had slowed down.

2. The fight or flight response that you were experiencing during the traumatic event can get quickly paired with cues (things in the environment that didn't have any particular meaning before).

   Later, when you're exposed to those cues, you may have another fight or flight response. Your nervous system senses the cue, then your body reacts as if you're in danger again.

   These reactions fade over time—*as long as you don't just avoid those cues*. However, your body won't learn that these aren't real danger cues if you just avoid them. You need a chance to learn when you're actually in danger without false alarms going off.

3. You may start to have thoughts about danger that are based on the reactions inside you—rather than the actual realistic danger of those situations.

---

*Adapted from Resick, P. A., Monson, C. M., & Chard, K. M. (2007). *Cognitive processing therapy: Veteran/Military version*. Washington, DC: Department of Veterans Affairs. May not be reproduced without permission.

THE STORIES OF TRAUMA

 **Handout**

If you can identify a traumatic event, take a few moments to make some notes about why you think this traumatic event occurred. For example: *My buddy died because I wasn't careful enough* or *I have done so many bad things in my life that I deserved this.*

You are *not* being asked to write specifics about the traumatic event. Write about what you have been thinking about as the cause of this event.

When you are done, we will discuss examples in the group. We want to make sure that no one in this group holds on to a distorted reason for why bad things have happened in their lives.

TRAUMATIC EVENT:

THIS HAPPENED BECAUSE . . .

May not be reproduced without permission.

HOMEWORK

 **Handout**

If you can identify a traumatic event, can you give three examples of "re-experiencing" (feeling like it's happening all over again) in your own life since the event?

1.

2.

3.

If you can identify a traumatic event, can you give three examples of intense emotions/physical reactions in your own life since the event?

1.

2.

3.

If you can identify a traumatic event, can you give three examples of avoiding something, feeling numb, or feeling disconnected from other people in your own life since the event?

1.

2.

3.

May not be reproduced without permission.

Session 4

MINDFULNESS AND GRATITUDES

Materials

Mindfulness in Everyday Life
Sumanai!

Program

1. Ask each group member to report one "gratitude."

2. Focus on the "mindfulness" exercise for 1 minute.

3. Review the homework from the previous week.

4. Review the *Weekly Check-Ins* and use these to help guide the group discussion in the first half of the group.

5. Discuss with the group members any experiences they have had with anything even remotely related to meditation: yoga, hypnosis, prayer, martial arts, transcendental meditation, and so forth. Explain that every meditation approach involves two primary tasks: to deepen and regulate breathing, and to clear and focus the mind.

6. Review the *Mindfulness in Everyday Life* handout. Choose some of the exercises and practice them in the group.

7. Review *Sumanai!* Ask each group member to write down his answers for one person, then go around the room and share the responses. Ask each group member to practice saying this to the person, using the basic script outlined in the exercise. Generate a discussion about how it feels to do this, including both the positive feelings and the resistance to it.

MINDFULNESS IN EVERYDAY LIFE*

 **Handout**

If you let cloudy water settle, it will become clear. If you let your upset mind settle, your course will also become clear.

From Jack Kornfield, *Buddha's Little Instruction Book* (New York: Bantam Books, 1994).

Mindfulness is a form of self-awareness training adapted from Buddhist mindfulness meditation. It has been adapted for use in treating depression, especially preventing relapse and for assisting with mood regulation.

It has been described as a state of being in the present, accepting things for what they are, that is, nonjudgmentally. It was originally developed to assist with mood regulation and relapse prevention in depression and has been found to have considerable health benefits.

These exercises are designed to introduce the principles.

SOME MINDFULNESS TECHNIQUES TO PRACTICE

One-Minute Exercise:

Sit in front of a clock or watch that you can use to time the passing of 1 minute. Your task is to focus your entire attention on your breathing, and nothing else, for the minute. Have a go—do it now.

Mindful Eating:

This involves sitting down at a table and eating a meal without engaging in any other activities—no newspaper, book, TV, radio, music, or talking. Now eat your meal paying full attention to which piece of food you select to eat, how it looks, how it smells, how you cut the food, the muscles you use to raise it to your mouth, the texture and taste of the food as you chew it slowly. You may be amazed at how different food tastes when eaten in this way and how filling a meal can be. It is also very good for the digestion.

Mindful Walking:

While you walk, concentrate on the feel of the ground under your feet and on your breathing while walking. Just observe what is around you as you walk, staying IN THE PRESENT. Let your other thoughts go: just look at the sky, the view, the other walkers; feel the wind, the temperature on your skin; enjoy the moment.

De-stressing Exercise:

Bring yourself into the present by deliberately adopting an erect and dignified posture.

Then ask yourself: "What is going on with me at the moment?"

You simply allow yourself to observe whatever happens. Label any thoughts that you have and then leave them alone . . . just be prepared to let them float away. Attend to your breathing or simply take in your surroundings instead.

---

*Courtesy of http://www.blackdoginstitute.org.au. May not be reproduced without permission.

Besides thoughts, there may be sounds you hear and bodily sensations that you are aware of. If you find yourself constantly elaborating on thoughts, rather than labeling them and returning to the neutral, remember to observe your breathing.

When emotions or memories of painful events occur, don't allow yourself to become caught up by them.

Give them short labels such as "that's a sad feeling" or "that's an angry feeling" and then just allow them to drift or float away. These memories and feelings will gradually decrease in intensity and frequency.

More important, you will begin to identify yourself as an objective observer or witness rather than a person who is disturbed by these thoughts and feelings. This requires practice but can then be used whenever you are stressed.

Associated Breathing Exercise:

Stay with any distressing thoughts for a few moments. Then, as you let them float away, gently redirect your full attention to your breathing.

Pay attention to each breath in and out as they follow rhythmically one after the other. This will ground you in the present and help you to move into a state of awareness and stillness.

*SUMANAI!**

 **Handout**

Sumanai! is the Japanese word for "This is not finished!" It is a way of acknowledging and accepting an obligation when you receive an act of kindness from someone. Instead of saying "thank you" (which is what we are all trained to say), *Sumanai!* means that we wish to continue the cycle by offering something in return. And, in Japan, this means that the other person now feels connected to us in a positive way. This leads to the experience of *ninjyo*: the feeling of secure, permanent connection with all other human beings.

Choose one person who has been very important in your life (excluding your spouse or partner). Write down the three most important things that this person has done for you.

Next, practice saying these thoughts to this person by role-playing in the group. Tell this person the following:

> *I still remember your kindness.*
> *I am still very much connected with you because of what you have done for me.*
> Sumanai!—*this is not finished.*

---

*Adapted from Bankart, P. (2006). *Freeing the angry mind*. Oakland, CA: New Harbinger Publications. May not be reproduced without permission.

HOMEWORK

Handout

1. Pick three other people in your life. Write down the three most important things that each person has done for you.

Person #1:

a.

b.

c.

Person #2:

a.

b.

c.

Person #3:

a.

b.

c.

2. If you choose to, either tell the person directly using the message you practiced in the group:

> *I still remember your kindness.*
> *I am still very much connected with you because of what you have done for me.*
> *Sumanai!—this is not finished.*

or send it in a letter or e-mail.

May not be reproduced without permission.

Session 5

SELF-TALK AND PERSONAL STORIES

Materials

Bad Rap
Bad Rap Quiz
Examples of Anger-Producing Self-Talk

Program

1. Ask each group member to report one "gratitude."

2. Focus on the "mindfulness" exercise for 1 minute.

3. Review the homework from the previous week.

4. Review the *Weekly Check-Ins* and use these to help guide the group discussion in the first half of the group.

5. Introduce a basic working model of "self-talk." Use the ABCDE model (explained below), emphasizing how the way we interpret events can determine the way we feel and act (from Wexler, 1991a).

   a. **Objective Event**: This is the initial event. Your wife or girlfriend comes home and says, *I hate my job!*

   b. **Self-Talk**: You might say to yourself: *She's trying to tell me that she doesn't want to work and that I should be making more money so she shouldn't have to!*

   c. **Feelings and Behavior**: If you interpreted it this way, you would probably be critical of her, or act defensive, or sulk, or worry. Maybe you would say to her: *Quit complaining! You think you're the only one who has it tough?*

   d. **New Self-Talk**: Maybe there was another way to interpret what she said. Maybe she was just tired and needed some support, like we all do. Maybe it was not intended as a message or critical comment. You might be saying to yourself, *She sounds like she's had a rotten day. What can I do to help?*

   e. **New Feelings and Behavior**: If you interpreted it this way, you might say: *Let's talk about it.* Or you might try to cheer her up. Or you might just whisk the kids off into another room and let her be alone for a while. Your response would be based on what you thought she might need, rather than defending yourself against a perceived attack.

6. Now explain the seven categories of *Bad Rap*. Teach the names of the categories and go through the different examples. Ask the group members to come up with examples of their own.

7. Quiz group members with the *Bad Rap Quiz*, to make sure that they get the idea. Try turning this into a Family Feud contest, with different teams competing for the right answer. If one team identifies the correct category for the statement, award a point. This team then has the opportunity to rephrase the statement so that it reflects "productive" or "realistic" self-talk, worth an additional point. If a team answers incorrectly, the other team can try, until one of the teams gets it right. Make sure that they learn how to revise the "faulty" self-talk into sentences that would be more "realistic" self-talk.

   This is designed to be entertaining and engaging, with one primary purpose. This purpose should be repeated and emphasized throughout this session and others: *We want you to see how powerful your self-talk is in determining your emotions and your behaviors in any situation. And we want you to see that it is possible, in a lot of these situations, to change the self-talk and end up with emotions and behaviors that do not mess you up so much. This is another example of making YOU powerful—not over others, but over yourself.*

8. Review *Misinterpretations*. Discuss the wide range of possible self-talk in response to the vignettes and how different outcomes and behaviors inevitably follow.

BAD RAP*

 **Handout**

1. **BLACK AND WHITE:** Seeing things as all or nothing. Beware of words like "never," "always," "nothing," and "everyone."

   Real men don't admit their mistakes.
   You're either on my side or you're not.

2. **MINIMIZING:** Downplaying your achievements.

   Even though I finally made supervisor, it's no big deal.
   I did well, but so did a lot of other people.
   My counselor just gives me good feedback because she's paid to say it.

3. **MINDREADING:** Assuming that others think something without checking it out.

   I know my boss hates me—he gave me a dirty look.
   She's avoiding me—she must be pretty mad.
   My girlfriend didn't call me today—she must not care about me.

4. **AWFULIZING:** Predicting that things will turn out "awful" for you.

   My boss will never trust me again.
   I know I'm not going to make it through this place.
   Wow, he is so good at that—I'll never be able to do it that well!

5. **ERROR IN BLAMING:** Unfairly blaming yourself—or others.

   It's all my fault, or *It's all their fault.*
   It's my fault my son is shy.
   You always mess everything up for me.

6. **DOWN-PUTTING:** Making too much of your mistakes (opposite of **MINIMIZING**).

   I failed this test; I must be dumb.
   I'm in counseling; there must be something really wrong with me.
   She doesn't like me; I must be ugly.

7. **EMOTIONAL REASONING:** Concluding that if you feel a certain way about yourself, then it must be true.

   Since I feel bad about myself, I must be a bad person.
   I feel rejected, so everybody must be rejecting me.
   Since I feel guilty, I must have done something wrong.

---

*Adapted with permission from Wexler (1991). May not be reproduced without permission.

BAD RAP QUIZ*

 **Handout**

1. The counselor told me I'm doing better, but I know he tells that to everybody. (2)

2. Ever since Linda hurt me, I know redheads can't be trusted. (1)

3. Nothing's ever going to work out for me. (4)

4. It's your fault we never do anything fun. (5)

5. My parents got divorced; it must have been something about me. (5)

6. I sometimes don't get things right so I must be lazy or stupid. (6)

7. I feel lonely, so I guess nobody likes me. (7)

8. That supervisor shows me no respect; nobody in this organization cares a damn about me. (1)

---

*Adapted with permission from Wexler (1991). May not be reproduced without permission.

EXAMPLES OF ANGER-PRODUCING SELF-TALK

 **Handout**

She called me a name.

This proves she doesn't show me respect.

I have to protect my honor.

I will show her what it feels like by calling her a name.

I have a right to pay her back for what she has done to me.

* *

 My supervisor is telling me I did something wrong.

 I feel embarrassed.

He is trying to embarrass me.

If I don't stand up to him, other people will think they can take advantage of me.

People do this to me all the time and I'm sick and tired of it.

Now is the time to prove to everyone that I must be taken seriously.

I will do whatever it takes to make sure everyone understands this!

May not be reproduced without permission.

HOMEWORK

 **Handout**

Record three examples of "bad rap" over the next week. Write down the negative self-talk and new self-talk that would have been more realistic or productive.

1. SELF-TALK

NEW SELF-TALK

2. SELF-TALK

NEW SELF-TALK

3. SELF-TALK

NEW SELF-TALK

May not be reproduced without permission.

Session 6
THE BROKEN MIRROR

Materials

Affliction video ("Halloween" scene begins at 13:40 and ends at 19:20)
Broken Mirror Sequence

Program

1. Ask each group member to report one "gratitude."

2. Focus on the "mindfulness" exercise for 1 minute.

3. Review the homework from the previous week.

4. Review the *Weekly Check-Ins* and use these to help guide the group discussion in the first half of the group.

5. Explain the concept of the "broken mirror" (Wexler, 2004). Here is a sample explanation:

> Each of us looks for a response from the people most important to us. Based on the response, we might feel good about ourselves or just the opposite. It's like the other person is a mirror: You look into her eyes, hear her words, watch the body language, and it's like a GOOD mirror reflecting back a picture of yourself as somebody who is decent and lovable—or a BROKEN mirror image of someone who is a loser. It is completely normal and human to feel this way—it happens every day to all of us.
>
> Some people get into situations where they see broken mirrors all over the place. If your wife says she needs to work more shifts because the family needs more money, her words might be a broken mirror to you: Her behavior means you are not a good-enough provider!
>
> In the following video, from the movie Affliction, let's watch what happens with the main character and his daughter. He has grown up with a very abusive father, and he is trying to be a better man. But he is only partly successful.
>
> In this scene, his 10-year-old daughter is living with his ex-wife. He has arranged for his daughter to spend the Halloween weekend with him, and he has a picture in his head of having a great time together. At some point, he has a broken mirror experience and he doesn't handle it very well. See if you can identify what she does that leads to the broken mirror for him—and how he handles it.

100

6. Play the scene from *Affliction* at the Halloween party, where Jill calls her mother to pick her up because she is not having a good time.

7. Lead a group discussion with the following questions:

> *Can someone describe the feeling that Wade (the father) had during the scene?*
> *What did Jill do that broke the mirror for her father?*
> *Did she intentionally try to make him feel bad?*
> *What did she do to try to remind him that this did not have to be a broken mirror for him?*
> *What did he do in response?*
> *Do you recognize yourself in this scene?*

8. Now present the *Broken Mirror Sequence* handout. Explain that this is the way men often experience the build-up of anger and explosiveness.

THE BROKEN MIRROR SEQUENCE*

 **Handout**

Once you see (or think that you see!) the broken mirror, a destructive sequence often follows. The sequence goes like this:

EVENT: Something happens in your life.

BROKEN MIRROR: You interpret it as negative and as a statement that there is something wrong with you.

BAD FEELINGS: You feel bad—but don't have the words or language to describe your feelings very well.

EMOTIONAL FLOODING: The bad feelings "flood" you.

TAKING ACTION: You feel the need to DO SOMETHING to make the bad feelings go away: either escape/withdraw, or retaliate against the person who (in your mind) is responsible for making you feel bad

According to this model, when you experience unbearable feelings—like hurt, shame, helplessness, fear, guilt, inadequacy, and loneliness—you will frequently feel overwhelmed. So you need to defend against these feelings, although these defenses do not provide much of a solution:

placing blame and denying responsibility on her: *"Why do you make me feel so bad about myself?"*

controlling everything and everyone in the vicinity: *"I want you all to get out of your rooms and clean up this house now—or else!"*

using alcohol or drugs to temporarily take away the pain

seeking excitement to distract from the bad feelings: *"I'm going to go get laid by someone who really knows how to make a man feel good!"*

When these defenses provide relief, they are reinforced, and you learn to keep using them. Although, of course, some event typically triggers a reaction, you must learn to tolerate a wider range of negative emotions without acting out.

Again: ***If you know what you are thinking and feeling, you are in a much more powerful position to truly be in charge of your own life.***

---

*Adapted from Wexler (2004). May not be reproduced without permission.

HOMEWORK

 **Handout**

Identify three "broken mirror" experiences over the next week. Note the situation and how this made you feel bad about yourself. We all have plenty of them.

1.

2.

3.

May not be reproduced without permission.

Session 7

MASCULINITY TRAPS AND TOUGH GUISE

Materials

Tough Guise video (begins at 10:15 and ends at 14:29/Chapters 6–8)
Men's Work video (put-downs and masculinity challenges, begins at 2:07 and ends at 11:57)
Men Are Supposed To. . .
Masculinity Traps

Program

1. Ask each group member to report one "gratitude."

2. Focus on the "mindfulness" exercise for 1 minute.

3. Review the homework from the previous week.

4. Review the *Weekly Check-Ins* and use these to help guide the group discussion in the first half of the group.

5. Explain that men engage in certain types of self-talk because of the roles in which they are placed. The primary roles, called "masculinity traps," are beliefs that men have to be in charge, must always win, and must always be "cool" and not express a range of feelings.

6. Play the *Tough Guise* video (begins at 10:15 and ends at 14:29/Chapters 6–8), starting at the "Upping the Ante" scenes and concluding with the conversation between the two Native American men. Discuss the pressure they both feel about how to "act like a man."

7. Play the *Men's Work* video: (put-downs and masculinity challenges, begins at 2:07 and ends at 11:57). Take a break at the point at which the exercise about "Men Are Supposed To . . ." appears on the screen. The screen will say STOP TAPE. Ask each of the group members to fill out the *Men Are Supposed To. . .* information. Return to the *Men's Work* videotape and listen to the examples that the actors recite. Generate a group discussion about these issues.

8. Review the *Masculinity Traps* handout. Encourage discussion by using the following questions:

> *Which of these masculinity traps do you recognize in yourself?*
> *Would you like your son to grow up with these masculinity traps? Why or why not?*
> *How do men suffer when they are stuck with these masculinity traps?*
> *What are some of the positive aspects of these beliefs?*

MASCULINITY TRAPS*

 **Handout**

As you review the self-talk that represents masculinity traps, ask yourself the following questions:

1. Which of these masculinity traps do you recognize in yourself?

2. Would you like your son to grow up with these masculinity traps? Why or why not?

3. How do men suffer when they are stuck with these masculinity traps?

4. What are some of the positive aspects of these beliefs?

"I can never show my feelings. Always be tough."

"Never show any weakness."
"Never do anything 'feminine.'"
"I have to be in control at all times."

"I must win."

"I must be successful at everything!"
"Don't back down from a fight."
"Always try to win arguments."
"Be on top by finding fault in others."
"Real men solve problems by force."

"My possessions and success are the measure of who I am."

"My value equals my paycheck."
"My car and my clothes and my house prove what kind of man I am."

---

*Adapted with permission from Daniel G. Saunders, PhD. May not be reproduced without permission.

MEN ARE SUPPOSED TO. . .

 **Handout**

Men are supposed to be . . .

1.

2.

3.

4.

Men are supposed to do . . .

1.

2.

3.

4.

Men are supposed to have . . .

1.

2.

3.

4.

Men are *not* supposed to . . .

1.

2.

3.

4.

May not be reproduced without permission.

HOMEWORK

 **Handout**

As you review the self-talk that represents masculinity traps, write your answers to the following questions:

1. Which of these masculinity traps do you recognize in yourself?

2. Would you like your son to grow up with these masculinity traps? Why or why not?

3. How do men suffer when they are stuck with these masculinity traps?

4. What are some of the positive aspects of these beliefs?

May not be reproduced without permission.

Session 8

MASCULINITY TRAPS: GUIDELINES FOR GOOD MEN

Materials

The Great Santini video (high school basketball game begins at 1:03:22 and ends at 1:12:18)
Relational Heroism
Guidelines for Good Men

Program

1. Ask each group member to report one "gratitude."

2. Focus on the "mindfulness" exercise for 1 minute.

3. Review the homework from the previous week.

4. Review the *Weekly Check-Ins* and use these to help guide the group discussion in the first half of the group.

5. Play *The Great Santini* video (the scene with the high school basketball game begins at 1:03:22 and ends at 1:12:18). Discuss the ways in which the son has become oppressed by his father's warped attitudes about masculinity.
   Consider these questions:

   Do you think Ben was more afraid of his father, or did he think that maybe his father's way was right?
   What options did Ben have? What could he have done differently? Could he have done anything differently without feeling "punked"?
   What was the difference between the coach's influence and the father's influence?

6. Review the *Relational Heroism* handout and discuss.

7. Review the *Guidelines for Good Men* handout and discuss.

RELATIONAL HEROISM

 **Handout**

Every day, people are heroes—not just in the obvious way of fighting tough wars or rescuing burning bodies from the World Trade Center or making tough decisions in the workplace, but rather by the ways they behave in their relationships.

We call these acts "relational heroism" (Real, 1997). Think of it this way: In a combat zone, we call someone heroic when he or she acts in a way that puts himself or herself at risk or when he or she makes a very tough decision for the greater good.

So, when you decide to put aside your own needs or hurt feelings in your relationship or with your kids for the greater good, you are being a hero. A "relational hero." And if you do this over and over again, you get into the Relational Hero Hall of Fame.

Preston was in the midst of a very rocky period in his marriage where the future was very much in doubt. He began talking to his wife about a vacation he was hoping they could go on almost a year away. She looked at him and said, half-joking and half-serious, *"Well, you're assuming a lot, aren't you?"* Preston remembers reacting this way: *Sharice made that crack about "Well, you're assuming a lot, aren't you?" and I just shut down, like I always do. I just felt so hurt. Same old stuff. But it didn't take me too long before I turned to her and told her that her comment had really hurt me, and I asked her, sort of nicely, why she had said it. And we actually had a conversation about the whole thing. I guess that's sort of the "relational hero" thing we've been talking about, isn't it? I guess I'm doing pretty well.*

In the movie *High Fidelity*, the main character, Rob, has a long history of failed relationships and a long history of selfish behaviors that contribute to these failures. He was very skilled at putting together mixtapes of carefully selected songs for a woman he was interested in—but he would only pick songs based on what he thought she *should* be listening to and was never able to see any woman as she really was, only as he wanted her to be.

Finally, after more and more errors and grief, he matures and has a breakthrough. He makes a mixtape for the new love of his life, Laura, which he describes like this: *. . . and I start to compile in my head a compilation tape for her, something that's full of stuff she's heard of, and full of stuff she'd play. Tonight, for the first time ever, I can sort of see how it's done* (Hornby, 1995, p. 323).

The task is so simple, yet it took him years to prepare for it. That's "relational heroism." It's not bold and dramatic to the outside observer, but it means so much.

May not be reproduced without permission.

GUIDELINES FOR GOOD MEN

 **Handout**

1. Think of the changes that you are being called upon to make as actions of "real men" and "relational heroes." Think about this in men's language like "taking charge," "becoming powerful," and being "captain of your own ship."

2. Take personal responsibility. You are not a victim of a bad childhood, life stress, or a nagging girlfriend. Real men don't make excuses.

3. Learn to tolerate distress. Feeling bad is not necessarily a cause for escape, avoidance, or immediate corrective action. Real men can handle negative affect by talking and thinking—and only then by taking possible smart actions.

4. Be very careful how you describe the events in your relationships. Take responsibility for your moods. Just because you feel injured or self-doubting does not necessarily mean that your partner has *tried* to make you feel that way.

5. Even when you have done something destructive in a relationship, you are still a "good man behaving badly" or a "good man acting cluelessly." Build the good man part while you analyze and correct the behaving badly part.

6. Pay attention to your possibly excessive attachment to the "look of love."

7. Keep a running list of times when you are tempted to act badly in a relationship but instead find a different way. These can serve as nuggets of hope and models to guide you in the future.

8. Do whatever you can to let the other key people in your relationships (partners and children) know that you believe in them and appreciate what they are going through—even if you do not always like their actions.

9. Be a responsible leader and bystander. Don't laugh and implicitly approve of other men who mistreat women or children.

10. Think of your kids all the time. Act in ways that you want them to model throughout their lives.

11. Take a chance. When you sense that the woman in your life needs emotional support or needs to hear more about you, talk to her. Admit if you feel helpless or don't know what to say or do.

12. Take care of your side of the street, even when you believe that she or he or they are not taking care of hers or his or theirs.

13. Take a chance. Try talking to other men about some of your feelings. Reveal not just complaints, but your actual fears, self-doubts, and worries. Tell them about things you have done or said in your relationships that you regret.

14. I know this is not easy, but try learning how to validate yourself, instead of needing a woman to validate you. Or try to find other ways to take in this validation that neither lead you to withdraw emotionally from her nor threaten your primary relationship. In other words, remember that it is healthy to need, unhealthy to need excessively, and essential to do nothing that is fundamentally disrespectful to someone you love and need.

May not be reproduced without permission.

HOMEWORK

 **Handout**

Review *Guidelines for Good Men*. Add one more that you would want to pass on to other men:

May not be reproduced without permission.

Session 9

JEALOUSY AND MISINTERPRETATIONS

Materials

> *Jealousy: Taming the Green-Eyed Monster*
> *Misinterpretations*

Program

1. Ask each group member to report one "gratitude."

2. Focus on the "mindfulness" exercise for 1 minute.

3. Review the homework from the previous week.

4. Review the *Weekly Check-Ins* and use these to help guide the group discussion in the first half of the group.

5. Explain the points made in the first part of the *Jealousy* handout. One of the strongest, most consistent traits of people who act abusively in relationships is jealousy. Sometimes the jealousy is based on reality and sometimes it is entirely fantasy— stemming from the insecurity of the person or distortions based on use of alcohol or other drugs.

    Depression, anxiety, insecurity, and shame can all make someone more sensitive to perceptions of threat in their intimate partner relationship.

6. Discussion Questions:

    Have you had thoughts or feelings similar to any of the people in the stories?
    What have you found that works to reduce jealousy?
    What constructive self-talk can you use to combat jealousy?
    How would you respectfully ask your partner for behavior change to reduce jealousy?

7. Review *Misinterpretations*. Discuss the wide range of possible self-talk in response to the vignettes and how different outcomes and behaviors inevitably follow.

JEALOUSY: TAMING THE GREEN-EYED MONSTER*

 **Handout**

Jealousy is one of those emotions that can tie our stomach in knots in a hurry. It is completely normal to feel a little jealous from time to time even in the healthiest of relationships.

However . . . jealousy becomes a problem

> when you spend too much energy worrying about losing a loved one
> when you let jealousy build and you try to control someone else through aggression
> when you stifle a relationship by placing extreme restrictions on your partner

Military trauma is another factor that can contribute to irrational jealousy. Depression, anxiety, insecurity, and shame can all make someone more sensitive to perceptions of threat in an intimate partner relationship.

Pete got himself really worked up whenever he went to a party with his wife, Tania. Other men were very friendly to her, and she was very friendly and outgoing herself. Pete was afraid that she would find another man more attractive and exciting than he was. He usually picked some sort of fight with her after the party, without ever telling her what he was really upset about.

One day after one of these fights Pete was thinking about how upset he made himself with jealousy. He tried to look at the situation in a more objective way—the way an outside observer would. After a while he was able to say to himself: *"My wife is very attractive, but that doesn't mean I'm going to lose her. She hasn't given me any reason to doubt her. My fears and anger come from doubting my self-worth. If other men like her, it only confirms what I already know!"*

Joe's jealousy was even stronger than Pete's. He would question his girlfriend at length when she came home, asking where she had been, who she had been with, and the details of her activities. He sometimes tore himself up wondering if she was having an affair. He would get urges to follow her everywhere or demand that she stay home. It seemed that the more he questioned her, the more he disbelieved her.

It was after hearing his friend talk about wanting to have an affair that Joe realized what was happening. The times when he was most suspicious of his girlfriend were the times when *he* was having sexual or romantic fantasies about *other women*. Now when he noticed jealousy, he asked himself: *"Am I just thinking that she's having these fantasies because I'm feeling guilty about my own?"*

Richard found that the best way for him to tame the jealousy monster was to let his wife know when he felt jealous. He felt very relieved being able to talk about it. Sometimes they could laugh about it together. Instead of responding with ridicule, his wife seemed to respect him more. Both of them went on to say what behavior from each other they could and could not tolerate—affairs, flirting, having friends of the opposite sex, and so forth. They were able to work out some contracts that specified the limits of the relationship.

What Pete, Joe, and Richard learned about taming jealousy was the following:

---

*Thanks to Daniel G. Saunders, PhD, for contributing these ideas. May not be reproduced without permission.

1. Some jealousy is normal, and it's best to talk about it rather than to hide it.

2. You can choose to see your partner's attractiveness and behavior in the most negative possible way—or you can turn it around and see it in a way that is not such a threat.

3. It will help you to ask: "*Is my jealousy coming from my guilt about my own fantasies or behavior?*"

4. You have the right to request a contract for some specific limits on your partner's behavior (not thoughts)—and she has the same right.

MISINTERPRETATIONS*

 **Handout**

Research shows that the way people think about their partners—the stories they tell themselves about the situation—plays a key role in launching abusive behaviors.

The main difference has to do with what is called reading negative intent, or making "hostile interpretations." A man who has been abusive is much more likely to think that his wife's or girlfriend's behavior was **intended** to hurt and humiliate him. He cannot just attribute her behavior to the fact that she is different from him, or that she wasn't thinking, or even that she may have been insensitive in that situation.

Discuss your self-talk *about your partner's intentions* in these situations:

You are at a social gathering and you notice that for the past half hour your wife has been talking and laughing with an attractive man. He seems to be flirting with her.

You are interested in sex and let your girlfriend know this. She isn't very interested but agrees to have sex. You begin to start things, making romantic moves. After a little while, you notice that she isn't very responsive; she doesn't seem to be very "turned on" or interested in what you are doing.

Men who are more likely to get abusive typically have "hostile interpretations":

> *"She was <u>trying</u> to make me angry."*
> *"She was <u>trying</u> to put me down."*
> *"She was <u>trying</u> to power trip me."*
> *"She was <u>trying</u> to pick a fight."*

Other men might have more neutral or even positive interpretations like these:

> *"I wish she would spend some more time with me here; I'll go over and talk with her."*
> *"She sometimes forgets that I'm not a good mixer; I'll talk to her about what I need the next time we go out."*
> *"I'm glad she's having a good time. It's a relief to me that I don't have to take care of her in social situations."*
> *"I'm kind of disappointed, but there are plenty of reasons why she doesn't want to have sex right now—no big deal."*

---

*Adapted with permission from Holtzworth-Munroe & Hutchinson (1993). May not be reproduced without permission.

HOMEWORK

 **Handout**

1. Record three experiences of jealousy over the next week. These can include anything from high levels (like seeing your wife or partner flirting with another man) to low (like observing your supervisor praise someone else). If you do not notice any this week, recall experiences from previous weeks.

   a.

   b.

   c.

2. Fill out the *"Who Is Responsible?" Questionnaire*. Prepare to discuss this in the group session next week.

May not be reproduced without permission.

Session 10

MISATTRIBUTIONS AND NEGATIVE INTERPRETATIONS

Materials

Men's Work *video* (spaghetti dinner scene begins at 19:16 and ends at 20:20)
"Who Is Responsible?" Questionnaire

Program

1. Ask each group member to report one "gratitude."

2. Focus on the "mindfulness" exercise for 1 minute.

3. Review the homework from the previous week.

4. Review the *Weekly Check-Ins* and use these to help guide the group discussion in the first half of the group.

5. Play the scene from the *Men's Work* video (spaghetti dinner scene begins at 19:16 and ends at 20:20), in which the husband assaults his wife after a frustrating day at work. Review the self-talk of the man in this scene. **This is the most important discussion point in this entire session.** Consider alternative self-talk that the husband might have used and discuss the different behaviors that might have resulted.

6. Review each of the items on the *Who Is Responsible? Questionnaire*. Use the group answers to generate a structured discussion about the negative stories people often tell themselves and how important it is to take full responsibility for one's own behavior. Keep referring back to Commandment #1.

"WHO IS RESPONSIBLE?" QUESTIONNAIRE

 **Handout**

James has never been very handy at fixing things around the house. At a barbecue with some of his friends and their wives, James's wife Lisa says, "Let's hope that this barbecue works because I know James will never be able to fix it!"

How likely is it that Lisa is trying to make him look bad in front of his friends?

1	2	3	4	5
EXTREMELY UNLIKELY	UNLIKELY	UNDECIDED	LIKELY	EXTREMELY LIKELY

If James starts yelling at Lisa, how much is she responsible for his reaction?

1	2	3	4	5
NOT RESPONSIBLE	SLIGHTLY RESPONSIBLE	UNDECIDED	MOSTLY RESPONSIBLE	EXTREMELY RESPONSIBLE

2. James is in a training program for auto mechanics. His teacher asks James to stick around after class because he wants to talk to him.

How likely is it that James is in trouble for something?

1	2	3	4	5
EXTREMELY UNLIKELY	UNLIKELY	UNDECIDED	LIKELY	EXTREMELY LIKELY

If the teacher tells James that his performance needs to approve and James gets mad, how much is the teacher responsible for James's reaction?

1	2	3	4	5
NOT RESPONSIBLE	SLIGHTLY RESPONSIBLE	UNDECIDED	MOSTLY RESPONSIBLE	EXTREMELY RESPONSIBLE

3. James comes home from work expecting a quiet evening at home with Lisa. But it turns out she's been called in to work and has fixed him some leftover spaghetti for dinner.

How likely is it that Lisa doesn't care about James or value him very much?

1	2	3	4	5
EXTREMELY UNLIKELY	UNLIKELY	UNDECIDED	LIKELY	EXTREMELY LIKELY

May not be reproduced without permission.

If James goes off on Lisa because she insists on going in to work, how much is she responsible for his reaction?

1	2	3	4	5
NOT RESPONSIBLE	SLIGHTLY RESPONSIBLE	UNDECIDED	MOSTLY RESPONSIBLE	EXTREMELY RESPONSIBLE

4. James's 10-year-old son Gabe is playing soccer and gets roughed up by a kid on the other team. Gabe runs off the field and won't go back in. James takes Gabe aside and tells him that he has to get back out there. Gabe refuses and starts crying.

How likely is it that Gabe is trying to make his father look bad?

1	2	3	4	5
EXTREMELY UNLIKELY	UNLIKELY	UNDECIDED	LIKELY	EXTREMELY LIKELY

If James starts yelling at Gabe, how much is Gabe responsible for his father's reaction?

1	2	3	4	5
NOT RESPONSIBLE	SLIGHTLY RESPONSIBLE	UNDECIDED	MOSTLY RESPONSIBLE	EXTREMELY RESPONSIBLE

HOMEWORK

 Handout

Identify one experience over the next week when you catch yourself using a "negative interpretation" about someone in your life. Record the "negative interpretation" and one alternative interpretation that might lead you to react differently.

Negative interpretation:

New Interpretation:

May not be reproduced without permission.

Session 11

SUBSTANCE ABUSE AND RELATIONSHIP ABUSE: WHAT'S THE CONNECTION?

Materials

Alcohol and Other Substances and Abuse: What's the Connection?
Alcohol and Other Substances Questionnaire
The Many Faces of Addiction
Why Do I Use?

Program

1. Ask each group member to report one "gratitude."

2. Focus on the "mindfulness" exercise for 1 minute.

3. Review the homework from the previous week.

4. Review the *Weekly Check-Ins* and use these to help guide the group discussion in the first half of the group.

5. Many people who hurt the ones they love have problems with alcohol. Some also have problems with other drugs, like pot and cocaine. It is unlikely, however, that alcohol and other drugs *directly* cause aggression. Rather, the causal connection appears to be indirect, acting through people's expectations, cultural norms, personalities, mind-sets, and environments. And during withdrawal, the person may become irritable and liable to lash out. Long-term abuse may contribute to paranoia and aggression.

    Some people who are abusive have a true addiction to alcohol or other drugs. Anyone who has relatives who are alcoholic should be told to be particularly cautious about drinking. It may be best to abstain from alcohol entirely. Blackouts are one sign of severe alcohol abuse. The group members need to be made aware that, while drinking heavily, they may seriously hurt a loved one or a stranger and never remember the event. Society can still hold them responsible for their behavior while drunk, because they put themselves at risk by taking the first drink.

6. Review *Alcohol and Other Substances and Abuse: What's the Connection?* and discuss.

7. Review the *Alcohol and Other Substances Questionnaire* and discuss.

8. Review and discuss *Why Do I Use?*

ALCOHOL AND OTHER SUBSTANCES AND ABUSE: WHAT'S THE CONNECTION?*

 **Handout**

Some people who hurt the ones they love have problems with alcohol. Some also have problems with other drugs, like pot, crack, and cocaine. Ours is a culture that often encourages the abuse of alcohol and the display of aggression under this influence. People under the influence sometimes do things impulsively they may not ordinarily do, and their judgment and control are impaired.

People use chemicals for many different reasons. On the questionnaires that follow, think about the reasons you use alcohol or drugs (if, in fact, you do). Then, identify whether alcohol or other drugs impair your judgment or cause you to become aggressive. Many people identify these themes as they think about these questions:

1. **Social Drinking.** There may be peer pressure and/or cultural pressure to abuse alcohol.

2. **Habit.** Many people think that socializing is only fun with alcohol use. Others believe the only way to unwind is through drinking. Drinking becomes routine.

3. **Psychological Dependency.** When alcohol use is well established, it's hard to imagine doing without it. By this stage, people have usually tried to stop—but there are too many reasons to keep using.

4. **Physical Dependency.** Once the person is physically addicted, withdrawal can have severe effects.

And ask yourself these questions as you think about the ways drugs or alcohol may be affecting your relationship problems:

Have you ever tried to cut back on your drinking or drug use?
Has anyone ever been annoyed about your drinking or told you that you have a substance problem?
Have you ever felt guilty for anything you've done under the influence?
Have you ever experienced memory lapses or "blackouts"?

Any "yes" answers indicate that alcohol use has probably impaired your ability to be fully in control of your life. Remember the 100% rule regarding responsibility. Alcohol problems are progressive—without help, they get worse. Can you really be 100% committed to being in control of your life and still abuse alcohol or drugs?

---

*Adapted with permission from Daniel G. Saunders, PhD. May not be reproduced without permission.

ALCOHOL AND OTHER SUBSTANCES QUESTIONNAIRE

 Handout

1. How often do you use alcohol or other drugs?
   a. Never
   b. Once every few months
   c. At least once a month
   d. At least once a week
   e. A few times a week
   f. Every day

2. What are the main reasons that you use alcohol or drugs?

   a.

   b.

   c.

3. What are the main "cues" for drinking or using drugs?

   a. Which people?

   b. What places/life events/situations (parties, work stress, sports games, etc.)?

   c. What emotions (sadness, anger, celebration, etc.)?

   d. What self-talk ("This isn't fair," "I deserve this," "It's time to have fun," "Nobody can control me," etc.)?

4. Name one time when you became more abusive or aggressive when using alcohol or drugs.

5. Has anyone ever told you that your alcohol or drug use is a problem?

May not be reproduced without permission.

THE MANY FACES OF ADDICTION*

 **Handout**

Addiction is not limited to alcohol, drugs, or cigarettes. It has many faces and shows up in many different ways. Some people have an addiction to one or two types of things, while other people may engage in many different kinds of addictive behavior: "cross addictions."

Here are the most typical addictions that ~~returning service members~~ ^{people} identify. Check all that apply to you:

Alcohol: Abuse or dependence
No _____   Somewhat _____   A Lot _____

Drugs: Abusing prescription medications, street drugs, "spice," "bath salts"
No _____   Somewhat _____   A Lot _____

Internet: "Surfing the net," chat rooms, on-line relationships
No _____   Somewhat _____   A Lot _____

Gambling
No _____   Somewhat _____   A Lot _____

Reckless driving/speeding/risk-taking behaviors (extreme sports/weapons/shoplifting)
No _____   Somewhat _____   A Lot _____

Sex: Soliciting prostitutes, masturbation, voyeurism, fetishism
No _____   Somewhat _____   A Lot _____

Smoking
No _____   Somewhat _____   A Lot _____

Video games/war games
No _____   Somewhat _____   A Lot _____

Exercise: Excessive working out, mixed martial arts, cage fighting
No _____   Somewhat _____   A Lot _____

Food: Overeating, anorexia, bulimia
No _____   Somewhat _____   A Lot _____

Relationships: Impulsively "falling in love"/serial relationships
No _____   Somewhat _____   A Lot _____

Reckless spending/shopping
No _____   Somewhat _____   A Lot _____

Workaholism
No _____   Somewhat _____   A Lot _____

_____
*Thanks to Dawn Galbo, PhD, and Marilyn Cornell, MFT, for development of this handout. May not be reproduced without permission.

WHY DO I USE?

 **Handout**

Think about the reasons that you use (or abuse) alcohol or other substances. Even if your use does not cause many problems in your life, it still serves some purpose. Check off on the list below the different reasons for your use of alcohol or other substances. We will discuss these in the next group session.

_____   To relax

_____   To feel more at ease in social situations

_____   Just because it tastes good

_____   Because my friends expect me to

_____   To have fun

_____   To avoid other people

_____   To feel more relaxed about having sex

_____   To avoid bad feelings (anger, depression, anxiety, loneliness, etc.)

_____   To have an excuse for getting rowdy

_____   To feel better about myself

_____   To stop worrying about problems

_____   To get a little buzzed

_____   To get really drunk

_____   To go to sleep

May not be reproduced without permission.

HOMEWORK

 **Handout**

Just for 1 week, keep track of how much alcohol you <u>consume</u>. Make notes of the day, the time of day, the situation, and the number of drinks. Remember that "one drink" is defined as one 6 oz. glass of wine, one 12 oz. beer, or 1½ oz. hard liquor.

May not be reproduced without permission.

Session 12
ACCOUNTABILITY

Materials

Accountability Defenses
Accountability Statement

Program

1. Ask each group member to report one "gratitude."

2. Focus on the "mindfulness" exercise for 1 minute.

3. Review the homework from the previous week.

4. Review the *Weekly Check-Ins* and use these to help guide the group discussion in the first half of the group.

5. Review *Accountability Defenses* and spend some time discussing individual answers. Make sure that all group members clearly understand each of the defenses and specifically identify some of their own.

6. Introduce the *Accountability Statement*. Review each line carefully. Assist the men in filling out their own form by using the group discussion. In this structured discussion, each group member should be able to identify specific ways when he has acted destructively in his primary relationship. This is purposely structured so that *anyone* could identify incidents that would fit this description. We are hoping to create a nondefensive atmosphere in which the men can openly recognize their abusive behaviors and clearly identify the ways in which—at that particular time—they justified them.

    If you have background on the incident history, either from the men's previous reports or from previous documentation, it can be helpful to remind them of examples of behavior destructive to the relationship. This review is designed to give the men time to examine their behavior and self-talk and to generate group discussion about the rationalization process. Refer to Commandment #1 (We are all 100% responsible for our own actions) throughout this discussion.

ACCOUNTABILITY DEFENSES

 **Handout**

Most people who behave destructively toward a partner find a way to justify it in their own minds. Even though they do not usually believe in being abusive toward a family member or partner, in certain situations they "make an exception."

Then, afterward, they figure out some way to make it okay, rather than simply saying the obvious: "I blew it. I crossed over a line, and it's nobody's fault but my own."

Here are some typical examples. Circle any that you have used and write in the specific words that you have said to yourself or others:

NO BIG DEAL: *I wasn't violent; all I did was slap her.*

INTENTION: *I didn't mean to hurt her—I just wanted her to understand!*

SELF-EXPRESSION: *It was <u>my</u> turn to let her know what I've been going through!*

INTOXICATION/LOSS OF CONTROL: *I was drunk; what can I say?/I just flipped out; I didn't even know what I was doing.*

PROJECTION OF BLAME: *It's her fault; if she hadn't pushed me, or nagged me, or spent too much money. . .*

DISTORTION OF ROLE: *I had to get physical with her for her own good—she was acting so crazy!*

May not be reproduced without permission.

ACCOUNTABILITY STATEMENT*

 **Handout**

We are making an assumption here—that all of you want the best in your relationships and do not want to be in abusive or destructive relationships. But something seems to come along and bring out behaviors in you that you thought you would never do.

But we are all still accountable for our own actions.

To be accountable means to acknowledge and take responsibility for one's actions. This handout will help you acknowledge destructive behavior in relationships. Although such behavior does not always turn into physical abuse, practically everyone—in almost *all* emotionally intimate relationships—behaves destructively at times. This is an opportunity to recognize past mistakes and demonstrate a desire to change them.

As you fill out this form, remember Commandment #1: "We are all 100% responsible for our own actions (even when it *feels* like someone else made us do it)." You will not be turning this in, but we will review this in group.

We are not asking you to admit to something that you did not do or to take responsibility for something that someone else has done.

I have acted in the following destructive ways toward my partner (circle each label that applies):

Verbal Abuse	Controlling Partner	Intimidation	Mind Games
Prop Destruction	Manipulating Kids	Threats	Forced Sex
Put-Downs	Stalking	Monitoring Mail/Phones	Sexual Put-Downs
Isolation of Partner	Controlling Money	Ignore/Withdraw	Affairs
Physical Restraint	Pushing	Slapping	Kicking
Throwing Things	Choking	Use of Weapons	Other

Other:_____

I take responsibility for these destructive behaviors. My behavior was not *caused* by my partner. I had a choice.

I have used the following to rationalize my destructive behaviors in this relationship (e.g., alcohol, stress, anger, "she was nagging me," etc.)

      1.

      2.

      3.

I recognize that my partner may be distrustful, intimidated, and fearful of me because of these behaviors.

---

*Adapted with permission from Pence & Paymar (1993). May not be reproduced without permission.

HOMEWORK

 **Handout**

Over the next week, pay attention to your self-talk and behaviors. Identify two examples in which you blamed someone else for your feelings or behaviors. You may use examples from the past if none occur to you this week.

1. SITUATION:

BLAMING THOUGHT:

2. SITUATION:

BLAMING THOUGHT:

May not be reproduced without permission.

Session 13

PUT-DOWNS FROM PARENTS

Materials

Put-downs from Parents
The Great Santini video (one-on-one basketball scene begins at 31:48 and ends at 40:23)
Boyz 'N the Hood video (father-son scene begins at 1:32:29 and ends at 1:37:28)

Program

1. Ask each group member to report one "gratitude."

2. Focus on the "mindfulness" exercise for 1 minute.

3. Review the homework from the previous week.

4. Review the Weekly Check-Ins and use these to help guide the group discussion in the first half of the group.

5. Before viewing the first video, present some basic ideas from Dutton's research about the relationship between male shame and domestic violence (see Dutton, 1995; Dutton, van Ginkel, & Strazomski, 1995).

   This research showed that the recollections of assaultive males were characterized by memories of rejecting, cold, and abusive fathers. In analysis after analysis, the scales measuring rejection were more important in influencing future abusiveness than those measuring physical abuse in childhood alone. The research showed that abusive men have frequently experienced childhoods characterized by humiliation, embarrassment, shame, and global attacks on their sense of self. Their parents would often publicly humiliate them or punish them at random.

   Typical shaming comments include the following:

   "You're no good."
   "You'll never amount to anything."
   "I should have had an abortion."
   "It's your fault that my life is a mess."

   People who have been exposed to shame will do *anything* to avoid it in the future. They blame others for their behavior. The result is a man who sometimes needs affection but cannot ask for it, is sometimes vulnerable but can't admit it, and is often hurt by some small symbol of lack of love but can only criticize.

When males have been rejected and shamed by their fathers, they become hypersensitive to situations that *might* be interpreted as shame situations in the future. So they are quicker to experience shame, and quicker to feel like they have to *do something* immediately to wipe it out. In these cases, men often blame their partners for making them feel this shame or humiliation, and they turn their rage on their partners to regain some sense of self. If it happens repeatedly with more than one woman, men may go from blaming her to blaming "them."

6. In presenting these ideas, try to use the word "put-down" rather than "shame" or "humiliation." The word "shame" is likely to lead to defensiveness and denial, and the word "put-down" can be interchanged to present the same ideas.

7. Play *The Great Santini* (begin at 31:48 and end at 40:23). Discuss the ways in which the father relentlessly attempts to humiliate his son because of his own insecurities. Guide the group discussion with the following questions:

    How does Ben feel in this situation?
    Would you want your son to feel like this?
    What was the intention of the Great Santini's actions? Was he trying to humiliate his son? Or was he trying to bring out the highest level of excellence in a way that turned out to be destructive?
    How do you feel about the role of Ben's mother in defending her husband?

8. After this general discussion, ask the group members to fill out the *Put-downs from Parents* questionnaire. **We have discovered that the men are much more forthcoming about reporting information on this questionnaire after watching this video.** These scales are not to be scored. They are only intended to help stimulate memories and discussion. Ask the men if they can identify experiences similar to Ben's in the movie.

9. Make sure to point out the connection between shame experiences from the past and self-talk in the present, particularly in relationship situations. The basic formula to emphasize is that men who were shamed (particularly by their fathers) as boys are especially sensitive to possible shaming situations as adults. So they are likely to tell themselves—more frequently than others—that they are being shamed. And they are likely to feel compelled to take some action to obliterate the perceived source of the shame.

    Can you identify ways in which you may be hypersensitive to criticism or put-downs because of your experiences as a child?
    What kind of self-talk can you use the next time you notice this?

10. To wrap up this session, play the clip from *Boyz 'N the Hood* (the father-son scene begins at 1:32:29 and ends at 1:37:28). In this scene, we see a strong, very masculine father whose steady attention to his son influences his son to make a mature decision—a contrast to the *Great Santini* scene we have already witnessed.

PUT-DOWNS FROM PARENTS*

 **Handout**

Please write in the number listed below (1–4) that best describes how often the experience happened to you with your mother (or stepmother, female guardian, etc.) and father (or stepfather, male guardian, etc.) when you were growing up. If you had more than one mother/father figure, please answer for the persons whom you feel played the most important role in your upbringing.

You might choose to share your responses with the group but that decision will be *completely* up to you. The more honest you can be as you describe yourself and your history, the more you will be able to benefit from this program.

1	2	3	4
Never Occurred	Occasionally Occurred	Sometimes Occurred	Frequently Occurred

	Father	Mother
1. I think that my parent wished I had been a really different kind of child.	_____	_____
2. As a child, I was physically punished or scolded in the presence of others.	_____	_____
3. I was treated as the "scapegoat" of the family.	_____	_____
4. I felt my parent thought it was my fault when he/she was unhappy.	_____	_____
5. I think my parent was mean and held grudges toward me.	_____	_____
6. I was punished by my parent without having done anything.	_____	_____
7. My parent criticized me and/or told me how useless I was in front of others.	_____	_____
8. My parent beat me for no reason.	_____	_____
9. My parent would be angry with me without letting me know why.	_____	_____

---

*Adapted with permission from Dutton, van Ginkel, & Strazomski (1995) from the *EMBU: Memories of My Upbringing* scale. May not be reproduced without permission.

HOMEWORK

 **Handout**

Fill out the *Put-downs from Parents* questionnaire again, this time from the perspective of one of your own children. If you do not have children, pick a child you know well and try to fill it out from his or her perspective.

May not be reproduced without permission.

Session 14
SHAME-O-PHOBIA

Materials

Good Will Hunting video (the "shame argument" scene begins at ~~1:30:23~~ 1:22:43 and ends at 1:34:52)

Program

1. Ask each group member to report one "gratitude."

2. Focus on the "mindfulness" exercise for 1 minute.

3. Review the homework from the previous week.

4. Review the *Weekly Check-Ins* and use these to help guide the group discussion in the first half of the group.

5. Introduce the *Good Will Hunting* video (the "shame argument" scene begins at 1:30:23 and ends at 1:34:52) about personal shame. In this scene, the main character reveals to his girlfriend his childhood history of abuse and neglect. He expresses it to her in a defensive rage, and it profoundly inhibits him from forming a positive relationship with a good woman who loves him.

6. Introduce the term *shame-o-phobia*. This is a handy way of identifying the profound fear many men have of the possibility of feeling shamed. *Shame-o-phobia* leads to desperate attempts to avoid possibly shaming situations. It also leads to defensive and aggressive reactions to the experience of shame.

7. Introduce the video: *This movie is about a young man, played by Matt Damon, who has grown up in rough neighborhoods on the streets of South Boston. He has been in and out of foster homes, physically abused, and has run with a real rough crowd. He finally meets a woman who is actually a good match for him, but he is terrified about getting closer to her. Watch what happens in this scene when she invites him to move to California with her. Watch how his fear of being more known by her leads to aggression toward her. This is a classic example of shame-based interpersonal violence.*

8. Play the video clip and discuss. Guide the discussion with the following questions:

   What takes place for Will in this scene which leads him to feel shame?

Can you identify the key words from his girlfriend that seem to trigger his shame reactions (scared, not honest, I want to help you)?
Do you think she is intending to shame him?
How does he react to the experience of shame?
How does the concept of "anticipatory shame" come into play?
Does his behavior qualify as abuse? What is the most hurtful thing he does in this scene?
Can you imagine other ways he could have handled this whole conversation? What self-talk would have been necessary for him to do this?

HOMEWORK

 **Handout**

Identify one time when you felt shamed by your wife or partner and describe how you handled this.

May not be reproduced without permission.

Session 15

SURVIVOR GUILT AND MORAL INJURY

Materials

Ordinary People video (the "survivor guilt" scene begins at 1:36:08 and ends at 1:45:39)
Survivor Guilt and Moral Injury

Program

1. Ask each group member to report one "gratitude."

2. Focus on the "mindfulness" exercise for 1 minute.

3. Review the homework from the previous week.

4. Review the *Weekly Check-Ins* and use these to help guide the group discussion in the first half of the group.

5. Introduce the concept of "survivor guilt." Explain that this is a particular form of guilt that some people have when they survive or succeed but someone else doesn't. This was originally identified in studying survivors of Nazi Holocaust camps, and we see this showing up in war situations. It even takes place in family situations when one child is healthy but another child has a disease or handicap.

6. Introduce the video clip from *Ordinary People* (the "survivor guilt" scene begins at 1:36:08 and ends at 1:45:39). Here is some suggested background and key themes for the group members to keep in mind:

   In the 1980 movie Ordinary People, *Conrad is the younger of two brothers in the "perfect" American family: white, upper middle class, country clubs, ritzy Chicago suburb. Perfect until the two boys are out on a boat on the lake and get caught in a storm, and Conrad's older brother drowns. Conrad, plagued with guilt about having survived when his brother died, deteriorates into depression and ultimately attempts suicide.*

   Conrad's belief is that he has committed the "crime" of surviving. Plus he keeps getting the message from his emotionally cold mother that he has failed to replace his brother. His grades drop, his mood plummets, he quits the swim team. And, most important for our discussion here, he becomes entangled in relationships where he is ob-

sessed with protecting others from having bad things happen to them. When he is offered a genuine positive opportunity by a girl who likes him, he is paralyzed with guilt and doubt. Conrad hurts her with his emotional withdrawal and never really explains why.

Conrad struggles with survivor guilt. He fears that he does not deserve success (or even to be alive) and that anything good for him will prove harmful to someone he loves and cares about.

Conrad is released from his survivor guilt when, after the crisis of losing a friend to suicide, he confronts his imaginary crime of surviving when his brother drowned. He finds a way to tell the story differently in his own head. His psychiatrist challenges him by asking what was the one wrong thing he did. What was his imaginary crime? Conrad blurts out: "I held on!" And then comes the new storyline, supplied by his psychiatrist: "Did you ever think that maybe <u>he</u> just wasn't strong enough?"

7. Review and discuss *Survivor Guilt and Moral Injury.* It is extremely important to remind the group members that it is helpful and human to feel guilt and re-morse—this can lead to being a better human being in the future. But it is deadly to feel shamed and hopeless—this leads people to give up or act out in despair. Remind them of this difference over and over!

SURVIVOR GUILT AND MORAL INJURY

 **Handout**

Survivor guilt is usually defined as a deep feeling of guilt often experienced by those who have survived some catastrophe that was harmful or took the lives of others:

> a feeling that they did not do enough to save the others who were harmed or died: *I should have known about that IED!*

> a feeling of being unworthy compared to those who were harmed or died: *It's an insult to my friend that I am still living because he really deserved to live.*

> a feeling of being responsible for something bad that happened: *I am being punished for bad things I have done.*

Moral injury is a special type of survivor guilt, often defined as perpetrating, failing to prevent, bearing witness to, or learning about acts that transgress deeply held moral beliefs and expectations:

> participating in or witnessing inhumane or cruel actions: *I shot women and children even though I wasn't sure they really posed a threat to us.*

> failing to prevent the immoral acts of others: *I watched what he did and I did nothing to stop him.*

> engaging in subtle acts or experiencing reactions that, upon reflection, transgress a moral code: *I actually enjoyed seeing those people die.*

If you tell yourself that the cause of what you did is *global* (*I would do these things even when I am not scared out of my mind*) and *internal* (*I guess this proves that I have no regard for human life*) and *stable* (*I will always be like this*), these beliefs will cause long-lasting moral injury. You will feel shame and anxiety about being judged.

Guilt is the horrible feeling we have when we have done something that we know is wrong. We can learn from guilt and repair ourselves as human beings: *I feel horrible about what I did and I am determined to learn from this.*

Shame, on the other hand, involves the "global" evaluation of the self: *I am a flawed and horrible person, and I will always be that way.*

The goal for anyone traumatized by *moral injury*? To understand how good people can sometimes make horrible mistakes and to forgive oneself for having an "imperfect self."

May not be reproduced without permission.

HOMEWORK

Handout

Describe what you would say to someone who is traumatized with *survivor guilt.* You can choose any of the following people:

a. yourself

b. someone you know

c. Conrad from *Ordinary People*

May not be reproduced without permission.

Session 16
SWITCH!

Materials

Switch!

Program

1. Ask each group member to report one "gratitude."

2. Focus on the "mindfulness" exercise for 1 minute.

3. Review the homework from the previous week.

4. Review the *Weekly Check-Ins* and use these to help guide the group discussion in the first half of the group.

5. Ask each group member to choose a disturbing situation from the past—"*perhaps the incident that got you here*"—or any other time when he has reacted with verbal or physical aggression. Remember that you are trying to assess the men's ability to examine personal responsibility—and new options—for abusive behavior.

   Lead the group member through the steps of "Switch!" This is a very important opportunity to assess how well the group member is able to examine himself and integrate new ideas. General instructions should be given, such as "*When role-playing this situation, combine all the skills you've learned so far: use relaxation skills, build up your self-esteem, challenge your 'bad rap,' and think constructively.*"

   The first two steps of "Switch!" are used to **identify the problem situation** and **identify the self-talk**. The first step is for the target member to describe the self-talk he was having building up to the problem situation. The next step focuses on what the person would like to develop as new coping self-talk: self-talk that would have led or would lead to a better outcome. The group members should help generate the new self-talk.

   Now the reframing begins. The target member is asked to **imagine that he is back in the problem situation**. The leader further instructs the target member to begin stating aloud the old self-talk that led to the destructive outcome. When the group leader gives the command, the group—in very loud unison—yells **"SWITCH!"**

Note: This is meant to be entertaining—and to provide a shock to the individual's typical self-talk patterns!

SWITCH!

Handout

1. *What went wrong?*
   a. Who was involved? When was it? Where was it? Describe exactly what was happening. Be specific and objective.
   b. Replay this like a movie. What exactly did you do and say?
   c. Other group members should help by asking questions so the "movie" is very clear.

2. *What was my self-talk?*
   a. What was your self-talk before, during, and after the situation?
   b. Freeze the frame of this movie so you can stop at different points and identify the self-talk.
   c. With the group's help, analyze the self-defeating or unproductive self-talk.

3. *What new, more productive self-talk could I have used?*
   a. What would you like to have said to yourself instead in this situation?
   b. Brainstorm with the group for alternative self-talk.

4. *The group yells "Switch."*
   a. Put yourself back in the problem situation.
   b. Practice the old self-talk out loud.
   c. When the group yells out **"Switch!"** try using your productive self-talk instead.

5. *What do you think? What does the group think?*
   a. Do you think this would have led to a different outcome?
   b. Do you *really* think you could use this new self-talk in the future? What might get in your way?

May not be reproduced without permission.

HOMEWORK

 **Handout**

Do your own "Switch!" exercise. Pick out another time when you wish you had not reacted the way you did in your relationship:

SITUATION AND YOUR REACTION

OLD SELF-TALK

NEW SELF-TALK

PREDICTED NEW REACTION?

May not be reproduced without permission.

Session 17

ASSERTIVENESS AND ASKING FOR CHANGE

Materials

Assertiveness
What Is Assertive Behavior?
Asking for Change

Program

1. Ask each group member to report one "gratitude."

2. Focus on the "mindfulness" exercise for 1 minute.

3. Review the homework from the previous week.

4. Review the *Weekly Check-Ins* and use these to help guide the group discussion in the first half of the group.

5. Review *Assertiveness* and *What Is Assertive Behavior?* as a way of giving basic education about assertiveness and of getting the men to become aware of their own degree of assertiveness.

   Write the Assertiveness definition on the board. **ASSERTIVENESS: TAKING CARE OF YOUR OWN NEEDS, THOUGHTS, AND FEELINGS IN A WAY THAT IS LEAST LIKELY TO MAKE THE OTHER PERSON FEEL ATTACKED OR ACT DEFENSIVE.**

   Refer back to this definition again and again as you review examples. In future sessions, give the group members a "pop quiz" on this definition.

   While discussing the four types of behaviors in the first handout, encourage the men to give examples. The group leaders should give other examples, then model and role-play the different assertive behaviors. Encourage the men to think of benefits of assertiveness for them personally or to the relationship.

   Remind the group members that these are tools, not rules. Sometimes it makes sense to be passive, and sometimes (like in self-defense situations) it even makes sense to be aggressive. These tools are all designed primarily for relationships that we *care* about—relationships that we want to preserve as respectfully as possible.

6. Review the *Asking for Change* handout. Role-play and discuss the examples. **Remind the group members that the theme here is respectful communication—which is more likely to bring about the relationship they truly want.**

ASSERTIVENESS

ASSERTIVENESS: TAKING CARE OF YOUR OWN NEEDS, THOUGHTS, AND FEELINGS IN A WAY THAT IS LEAST LIKELY TO MAKE THE OTHER PERSON FEEL ATTACKED OR ACT DEFENSIVE

1. **Assertive.** This behavior involves knowing what you feel and want. It also involves expressing your feelings and needs directly and honestly without violating the rights of others. At all times you are accepting responsibility for your feelings and actions.

   "It bothered me when you were late coming back from shopping, because I had to rush off to work."

2. **Aggressive.** This type of behavior involves attacking someone else, being controlling, provoking, and maybe even being violent. Its consequences could be destructive to others as well as yourself.

   "What the hell's wrong with you? All you ever think about is yourself!"

3. **Passive.** The person withdraws, becomes anxious, and avoids confrontation. Passive people let others think for them, make decisions for them, and tell them what to do.

   He feels resentful but doesn't express it or deal with it. He feels like it's useless: either he doesn't deserve any better, or nobody will ever listen to him anyway. Usually he will become depressed, and he may believe that his wife or partner is purposely trying to take advantage of him—but he does nothing about the situation.

4. **Passive-Aggressive.** In this behavior the person is not direct in relating to people and does not accept what is happening but will retaliate in an indirect manner. This type of behavior can cause confusion. The other person feels "stung" but can't be exactly sure how or why. And the person who has done the stinging can act like he has done nothing at all—and imply that the other person is just "too sensitive."

   The man acts cold to his girlfriend, then pretends like nothing's wrong when she asks him about it. Or a man who is feeling unappreciated by his wife "forgets" to give her a phone message. Or makes some "joking" comment about her weight!

May not be reproduced without permission.

WHAT IS ASSERTIVE BEHAVIOR?*

 **Handout**

1. Asking for what you want but not being demanding.

2. Expressing feelings.

3. Genuinely expressing feedback or compliments to others and accepting them.

4. Disagreeing, without being aggressive.

5. Asking questions and getting information from others.

6. Using "I" messages and "I feel" statements without being judgmental or blaming.

7. Making eye contact during a conversation (unless this is inappropriate in the person's culture).

EXAMPLES:

1. *Can you give me some feedback about how I handled the kids' homework tonight?*

2. *I feel embarrassed when you tease me about my weight in front of my friends.*

3. *Mom, I know you want us to call more often, but I don't think you realize how busy we both are.*

4. *Corey, I just saw your report card and I'm concerned. Let's sit down and talk about this together.*

5. *Sarah, I'd like to talk about this later after we've both cooled off.*

6. *I really care about you; let's work this out.*

*Adapted with permission from Geffner & Mantooth (1995). May not be reproduced without permission.

ASKING FOR CHANGE

 **Handout**

This is a communication technique for when you would like the other person to change something. The goal (as with all assertive communication) is to communicate clearly and respectfully in a way that is least likely to put the other person on the defensive. Why? Because it works.

Construct "I" messages by using these phrases:

When you . . . (just describe, don't blame)

I feel . . . (state the feeling) **because** . . . (explain in more detail)

> *Note:* Using the word *because* with an explanation can help by giving the other person more information to understand you.

I wish . . . (specify new behavior you want the other person to use instead)

And if you can do that, I will . . . (explain how the other person will benefit)

The different parts of the "I" message do not have to be delivered in exact order. The important thing is to keep the focus on yourself and to stay away from blame.

> *When you take long phone calls during dinner,*
> *I get angry because I begin to think you don't want to talk to me.*
> *I wish you would tell whoever's calling that you'll call back because we're in the middle of dinner.*
> *And if you can do that, I'll make sure not to hassle you about being on the phone later.*

> *When you don't come home or call,*
> *I get worried that something has happened to you.*
> *I would really like you to call me if you're going to be late.*
> *And if you can do that, I promise not to have an attitude when you get home.*

> *When you yell at me right in the middle of a busy time at work,*
> *I get so rattled that I end up making more mistakes.*
> *I wish that you would lighten up when you know that I'm busy.*
> *And if you can do that, I will be a lot easier to work with.*

CLASSIC MISTAKES:

1. Being too vague: *"When you are selfish . . ."*

2. Putting down character (*"You are so controlling!"*) instead of describing a specific behavior (*"Last night it bothered me that you gave me so many instructions about the kids"*).

3. Saying *I feel that you . . .* instead of *I feel* (emotion).

4. Not offering a specific and realistic new behavior (*"I want you to become a more outgoing person"*).

May not be reproduced without permission.

HOMEWORK: KEEPING TRACK

 **Handout**

Think about a situation that upset you during the week. Record the information below. As you think about it, record what you would *like* to have done in this situation.

Situation and Date	
Body Reactions (Physical Feelings)	
Self-Talk	
How I Felt (Emotions)	
What I Did	
The Best Way to Handle It	

May not be reproduced without permission.

Session 18

HANDLING CRITICISM

Materials

Handling Criticism

Program

1. Ask each group member to report one "gratitude."

2. Focus on the "mindfulness" exercise for 1 minute.

3. Review the homework from the previous week.

4. Review the *Weekly Check-Ins* and use these to help guide the group discussion in the first half of the group.

5. In all relationships, people become critical of each other—constructively or destructively. It is difficult for most people to deal with criticism, and in most cases they get defensive. A major part of communicating effectively is not only to give constructive criticism but also to receive criticism.

    The objective of this session is to teach skills in taking criticism in the most assertive, nondefensive fashion.

6. Give the group members the *Handling Criticism* handout. The opening sections, including the nonconstructive ways of dealing with criticism, can be portrayed in a humorous way. Use examples and role-playing when teaching both nonconstructive and constructive ways of handling criticism.

HANDLING CRITICISM*

 **Handout**

**EVERY DESTRUCTIVE AND DEFENSIVE RESPONSE IS DESIGNED TO SHUT DOWN
THE OTHER PERSON AND THE CONVERSATION. IF THESE ARE YOUR GOALS,
THEN YOU SHOULD CONTINUE TO USE THESE RESPONSES.**

**BUT IF YOUR GOAL IS TO HAVE A MORE RESPECTFUL RELATIONSHIP
WHERE BOTH PEOPLE GET HEARD, THEN YOU MAY NEED TO CHANGE.**

THE WRONG PATH: DESTRUCTIVE AND DEFENSIVE RESPONSES

Everyone is occasionally criticized. How you *handle* criticism is especially important in intimate relationships. It is not uncommon to react defensively, such as . . .

1. ***Avoid the criticism or critic.*** Ignore, change the subject, clown around, refuse to talk about it, be too busy, withdraw, or even walk away.

   When your wife says something critical to you, don't respond verbally. Just give her a look that says "go to hell"—and walk out of the room.

   When your daughter is trying to talk to you, look at the floor, stare into space, or just look through her. Avoid making direct eye contact.

   Shut down the conversation by saying, *I don't want to talk about this!*

   Suppose you are really late coming in to work and a co-worker is upset and wants to know where you have been. You could change the subject by talking about sports.

   Practice avoiding: Your wife says to you, *You don't help much with cleaning up around here.* How would you AVOID the criticism?

2. ***Deny the critical comment.*** Deny facts, argue, present evidence, do not take any responsibility for anything.

   I never said you were fat. I just said your dress looks tighter on you than it used to.

   Deny that it happened. *I wasn't drunk at the party.* Or act dumb: *I don't know what you're talking about, I don't understand.*

   Practice denying: Your girlfriend has made dinner for both of you. You told her you would be home at 6:30. After you come home an hour late from hanging out with your friends, she says, *I don't know why I bother to treat you well. You should have been home when you told me you would be!* How would you DENY the criticism?

---

*Adapted from Geffner & Mantooth (1995). May not be reproduced without permission.

3. *Make excuses.* Act very sorry but have an alibi or excuse, or make it sound like your behavior was no big deal.

> You were late to pick up your friend, so you go into detail about how the keys got lost, you had to search for them, and the baby is always losing everything. Your friend will soon just want to forget he or she ever said anything.

> Again you are late and your friend is upset. Make statements like, *Well, so what if we didn't get to the movie on time? Look at all the important things I have to take care of everyday.*

> To your wife: *So I spent a lot of time talking to that girl at the party; that doesn't mean I care about her. I was just being friendly. You're just overreacting because you're so insecure.*

Practice excuses: You are getting phone calls from an old girlfriend and not doing anything to discourage them. Your wife says, *You obviously care a lot more about her than you do about me. You tell her to stop calling this house!* How would you MAKE EXCUSES about the criticism?

4. *Fight back.* Attack and get even. Put the other person on the defensive. This can be aggressive (direct) or passive-aggressive (indirect).

> Suppose one of your employees says something about needing more help from you when things are busy at work. You can attack him for always bringing up subjects at the wrong time or saying it in the wrong way. Or you can attack his work habits, friends, productivity, and so forth. You could get even by forgetting to schedule him for the shifts he requested.

> *Why do you always bring these things up at the wrong time? Don't you know how stressed out I am?*

> *Why are you always such a complainer?*

> Or the extreme version of fighting back if somebody criticizes you in public or in your relationship: physically assault the person!

Practice fighting back: You drove home after having too many beers. Your wife says, *That was so stupid. Don't you even care about me or the kids?* How would you FIGHT BACK at the criticism?

HANDLING CRITICISM (*continued*)

Handout

THE RIGHT PATH: CONSTRUCTIVE RESPONSES

As you can see, all these ways of handling criticism can seriously hurt good communication and destroy relationships. Major arguments may develop because someone has been ignored, argued with, or attacked. Because the common responses to criticism are so destructive to communication and relationships, try these instead:

1. **Ask for details.** Criticisms are often vague or given in generalities. So if someone says to you, *You're being really lazy* or *I don't like the way you're acting* you can ask for details to find out exactly what he or she is talking about.

    Can you please tell me more?

    Would you please be more specific so I can understand?

Suggest possible complaints and ask whether these might be the problem. *Are you upset because I didn't pay enough attention to you at the party?*

Your wife or partner says, *You're rude.* Respond, *Yeah, sometimes I can be rude. I know that. But what have I done just now that sounds rude to you?*

2. **Agree with the accurate part of the criticism.** A second step to handling criticism effectively is to agree with the part of the criticism that is true.

Suppose you go to a movie and you liked the movie but your girlfriend criticizes you for liking it. Instead of getting defensive, say, *Yeah, I like these romantic comedies; I guess we have different taste in movies. Are you saying that you want to have more say in the kind of movies we see?*

3. **If she is right, then apologize!** This is the most mature and adult thing to do. There is no shame in acknowledging mistakes, as long as it is accompanied by a genuine effort to correct them.

GENERAL GUIDELINES FOR HANDLING CRITICISM:

1. Learn to see criticism as an opportunity to learn and grow.
2. Try to avoid being defensive.
3. Listen actively.
4. Watch nonverbal language.
5. Monitor physical and emotional cues.
6. Act, but do not react.

May not be reproduced without permission.

HANDLING CRITICISM (*continued*)

GETTING IT RIGHT

Practice constructive and mature responses to criticism in the same four situations:

1. Your wife says to you, *You don't help much with cleaning up around here.*

What's the best way to respond?

2. Your girlfriend has made dinner for both of you. You told her you would be home at 6:30. After you come home an hour late from hanging out with your friends, she says, *I don't know why I bother to treat you well. You should have been home when you told me you would be!*

What's the best way to respond?

3. You are getting phone calls from an old girlfriend and not doing anything to discourage them. Your wife says, *You obviously care a lot more about her than you do about me. You tell her to stop calling this house!*

What's the best way to respond?

4. You drove home after having too many beers. Your wife says, *That was so stupid. Don't you even care about me or the kids?*

What's the best way to respond?

May not be reproduced without permission.

HOMEWORK

 **Handout**

Write down an example of a situation when you thought that someone in your life was being critical. Write your feelings and whether the criticism was constructive or destructive. Describe exactly how you handled it: your self-talk, your feelings, and your response. Discuss how you might have handled it better.

Criticism:

Self-Talk:

Feelings:

Your Response:

Better Response:

May not be reproduced without permission.

Session 19

FEELINGS, EMPATHY, AND ACTIVE LISTENING

Materials

Expressing Your Feelings
Active Listening

Program

1. Ask each group member to report one "gratitude."

2. Focus on the "mindfulness" exercise for 1 minute.

3. Review the homework from the previous week.

4. Review the *Weekly Check-Ins* and use these to help guide the group discussion in the first half of the group.

5. Review the *Expressing Your Feelings* handout. Role-play the different situations. Review assertive and nonassertive ways of expressing feelings. Discuss the different ways we decide whether or not a situation is worth a response.

6. Review the *Active Listening* handout. Explain the basic concepts, then model and role-play active listening based on the different examples.

7. IMPORTANT: At the end of this session, make sure to prepare the group members for the *Wives and Partners* group session next week:

   Next week is a special theme, called the "Wives and Partners" group. As soon as you walk in the door, you will take on the role of your wife or partner, either current or the partner that you were with when this incident happened. You're all going to spend the whole group session, in character, as her. We've heard a lot about what's happened in your family from your point of view. Now we'd like to hear exactly how she feels and felt and what she goes through and went through. You'll be surprised how much you will learn!

EXPRESSING YOUR FEELINGS

 **Handout**

For each situation below:

> **Identify your feelings.**
>
> **Put into words how you might express your feelings. Remember to use "I feel" statements.**
>
> **Remember that you don't always have to respond. If you would choose to say nothing in any of these situations, describe your feelings.**

1. Your girlfriend was going to meet you downtown for lunch, and you have been waiting over an hour. She finally arrives and says she had a few errands to run before she came.

2. A friend of yours makes a "joking" comment about how your wife has "really put on some weight lately."

3. Your wife teases you in front of your friends about how much trouble you have trying to fix things around the house.

4. You are late getting home and your wife or partner demands an explanation, but as soon as you begin she interrupts and starts yelling and saying how inconsiderate you are.

May not be reproduced without permission.

ACTIVE LISTENING

Handout

Active listening is a communication technique that encourages the other person to continue speaking. It also enables you to be certain you understand what the other person is saying. It's a way of checking it out. It's called *active* listening because you not only listen but also *actively* let the other person know that you have really heard her.

A. ***Active listening involves paraphrasing.***

Paraphrasing is stating in your own words what you think the other person has said.

You sound really <u>(feeling)</u> about <u>(situation)</u>.

You must really feel <u>(feeling)</u>.

What I hear you saying is _____.

B. ***Active listening also involves clarifying.***

Clarifying involves asking questions to get more information.

Clarifying helps you hear more specifics about the situation and feelings.

Clarifying also lets the other person know you are interested in what he or she is saying.

So tell me what happened that got you so upset.

How did you feel when that happened?

C. ***Active listening often involves personalizing.***

1. *Personalizing* involves offering a personal example of feeling the same thing or being in the same situation.

   I think I know what you mean. I've been there too.

   I felt the same way when I lost my job. I think everyone does.

2. *Personalizing* helps the other person feel less alone, and it implies that someone else has experienced this and has recovered from it.

3. *Personalizing* can be harmful if you talk *too* much about yourself and steal the spotlight from the person who needs it.

   You think that was bad? Listen to what happened to me!

D. ***Active listening does <u>not</u> mean cheering up, defending yourself, judging the person, or just repeating back exactly what was said.***

All I ever do is the dirty work around here!
Oh, come on, it's a hot day, you're just in a bad mood, don't worry about it.

———————
May not be reproduced without permission.

You can't trust anyone around this place!
Now, now, it's okay. It's all going to be better—I'll take care of it for you.

I'm really worried that my family is going to be mad at me for dropping out of school.
You shouldn't feel that way.

I keep trying to talk to you about how to handle the kids and you never listen to me!
I'm in charge! No more discussion!

This place is really disgusting.
It sounds like you think this place is really disgusting.

Some keys to being a good active listener: Good eye contact, leaning slightly forward, reinforcing by nodding or paraphrasing, clarifying by asking questions, avoiding distractions, trying to really understand what was said.

HOMEWORK

 **Handout**

1. Record three examples of your *Active Listening* responses over the next week.

Situation:

You Said:

****

Situation:

You Said:

****

Situation:

You Said:

May not be reproduced without permission.

Session 20

INTIMACY TRAINING: WIVES AND PARTNERS GROUP

Materials

None

Program

1. Ask each group member to report one "gratitude."

2. Focus on the "mindfulness" exercise for 1 minute.

3. Review the homework from the previous week.

4. Review the *Weekly Check-Ins* and use these to help guide the group discussion in the first half of the group.

5. Many of the men in our groups have deficits in empathy. Their behavior might be quite different if they were genuinely aware of the effect of their behavior on the other people around them.

   You might consider saying something like this as an introduction to this session: *The reason that you are each here is because, at some point in the past, you have done something that felt hurtful to your wife or partner. We all have. At the time, you simply may not have been aware of how you were affecting your wife or partner or what it must have been like to be in her position. We'd like to help you gain more of that knowledge, so that the next time around you'll be better informed. If you knew then what you know now (or what you are now learning), you might have made other choices.*

6. The instructions are quite simple: *This is the Wives and Partners group. We have invited you all here today to hear your side of the story. We've heard a lot about what's happened in your family from your husband's or partner's point of view. Now we'd like to hear exactly how you felt and what you went through.* A group member describes an interpersonal conflict situation from the point of view of his partner. All the group members play the role of their own wives or partners. The entire 2-hour group session is conducted in this role-playing fashion.

   Each group member must describe exactly what his wife or partner is thinking or feeling—without sarcasm, without editorial comments, without trying to make

164

her look bad. The group should keep giving feedback until they think he has played the role just right and has **truly gotten inside the other person's shoes**.

The goal here is not problem solving, but understanding. It is also important to remind the men that gaining an empathic point of view does not necessarily mean agreeing with the other person, but simply understanding what it must feel like to be that person.

7. One way to structure this exercise is to make notes on the board during the check-in process. These notes describe the wife's or partner's point of view in the argument. Then use these for the empathy-training exercise. For example:

> *Carrie is suspicious because another woman has been calling me.*
> *Denise gets on my case about going off to play basketball.*
> *Nina insisted on watching her TV show even though she knew it was time for ESPN SportsCenter.*

8. Encourage all the group members to join in with questions and discussion of their fellow wives and partners.

HOMEWORK

 **Handout**

Write one paragraph (at least 100 words) as if you are your wife or partner. The subject is "Sometimes I Don't Trust My Husband (or Partner) Because . . ."

May not be reproduced without permission.

Session 21

FOUR HORSEMEN OF THE APOCALYPSE

Materials

Four Horsemen of the Apocalypse
Conflict With Respect

Program

1. Ask each group member to report one "gratitude."

2. Focus on the "mindfulness" exercise for 1 minute.

3. Review the homework from the previous week.

4. Review the *Weekly Check-Ins* and use these to help guide the group discussion in the first half of the group.

5. Research by Dr. John Gottman and his colleagues (Gottman, 2000) has helped us understand patterns in marital communication that are almost sure to doom a marriage. The *Four Horsemen of the Apocalypse* handout explains the basic principles and examples of these communication patterns. Use the handout as a discussion guide for understanding how this works. Ask the men to identify themselves and their partners in these examples.

   Make sure to (1) identify the self-talk patterns that govern these patterns and to (2) role-play alternatives for how to use different self-talk and different communications.

   Clearly highlight the following two main points:

   a. Review the definitions of the *Four Horsemen of the Apocalypse*. Emphasize that the men should be able to identify these patterns and to try and reduce them in their relationships.

   b. Discuss how the narratives that people have in relationships determine their emotional and behavioral reactions.

6. Review the *Conflict With Respect* model (especially the softened start-up rules) and role-play examples of each, including the "wrong" way of doing it. Use this session to review many of the communication principles the group has already learned.

FOUR HORSEMEN OF THE APOCALYPSE*

 **Handout**

ACCUSATIONS (CRITICISM): Complaints are expressed in a destructive manner, as an attack on the other person's character: *You're so thoughtless and self-centered!*

In a constructive complaint, the person states specifically what is upsetting her, and constructively criticizes the other person's action, not the person himself, saying how it made her feel.

CONTEMPT (DISGUST): Contempt is usually expressed not just in the words themselves but also in a tone of voice and an angry expression. Rolling the eyes. A look of disgust.

What distinguishes *contempt* is the *intention to insult* and *psychologically abuse* the other person. When contempt begins to overwhelm the relationship, one person tends to forget entirely the other person's positive qualities, at least when feeling upset. He can't remember a single positive quality or act.

DEFENSIVENESS: Defensiveness is the fighting-back response. Here the person refuses to take in anything the other person is saying. It is one arm of the typical "fight or flight" response.

Defensiveness feels like an understandable reaction to feeling besieged—this is why it is so destructive. The "victim" doesn't see anything wrong with being defensive, even though this attitude escalates a conflict rather than leading to resolution. Defensive people never say, *Maybe you're right* or *I see your point* or *Yeah, I get it. I think I owe you an apology.*

STONEWALLING: Stonewalling is the ultimate defense. The stonewaller just goes blank and withdraws from the conversation. This sends a powerful message: icy distance, superiority, and distaste. Don't confuse stonewalling with a Time-Out. A Time-Out communicates **respect**. The message is that the person cares enough about the relationship to take special efforts not to cause any further damage. And there is a very clear contract that the discussion *will* continue at a future time.

---

*Adapted from Gottman (2000). May not be reproduced without permission.

CONFLICT WITH RESPECT

 **Handout**

Arguments can be a useful way to solve problems, or they can be never-ending battles that can increase tension and the risk of abuse. The central theme here, as always, is *respect.* Can you offer your partner respect even when you're upset? The following guidelines can make a difference:

DANGEROUS: THE "NEGATIVE START-UP"

Why am I the only one who ever does any cleaning up around here!

It may seem true at the moment, but...

- it is an exaggeration of the truth.
- it does not honor the positive qualities of your partner.
- it is usually communicated in a hostile tone of voice.

INSTEAD: RULES FOR A "SOFTENED START-UP"

Be concise.
In the initial start-up complaint sentence, complain but don't blame.
Start with something positive.
Make statements that start with "I" instead of "you."
Describe what is happening, but don't evaluate or judge.
Talk clearly about what you need.
Be polite.
Express appreciation.
Don't store things up.
Restate your feelings in terms of the more vulnerable emotions.

I know you've been really busy with the kids, but I could really use some help getting the kitchen cleaned up.

HOW TO AVOID UNFAIR BEHAVIOR (DISRESPECT)

Do not use name calling or put-downs.
Do not drag up old wounds from the past.
Stay on track; do not go off in different directions.
Do not threaten or intimidate.
Do not assume that you will either win or lose this argument.
Do not save up all your gripes to dump on your partner all at once.
Be careful of "mind-reading" self-talk. Don't assume the most negative things about your partner. ASK!
Do not deny the facts. Come clean.
Do not gloat over a "victory" in getting your way.
Do not sulk, ignore, pout, withdraw, or give your partner the silent treatment.

May not be reproduced without permission.

HOMEWORK

 **Handout**

Practice the "softened start-up" three times. Record the results.

My "softened start-up" statement:

Response from my partner:

****

My "softened start-up" statement:

Response from my partner:

****

My "softened start-up" statement:

Response from my partner:

May not be reproduced without permission.

Session 22

INTIMACY TRAINING: TELLING YOUR TRAUMA STORY TO YOUR PARTNER

Materials

Hurt Locker video (the "vets returning home" scene begins at 1:57:20 and ends at 2:05:51/Chapters 17–18)
Telling Your Story

Program

1. Ask each group member to report one "gratitude."

2. Focus on the "mindfulness" exercise for 1 minute.

3. Review the homework from the previous week.

4. Review the *Weekly Check-Ins* and use these to help guide the group discussion in the first half of the group.

5. Play the video clip from *The Hurt Locker* (the "vets returning home" scene begins at 1:57:20 and ends at 2:05:51/Chapters 17–18), which shows the main character's inability to talk about his combat zone experiences and his inability to reintegrate into everyday life at home.

6. Lead a group discussion about issues related to "telling your story." Make it clear that we are talking about any kind of personal trauma (combat zone, childhood exposure to violence, traumatic loss, etc.)

   What are the benefits of telling your trauma story?
   Whom have you already told about your traumatic experiences?
   What are your fears about telling your story?
   What would make it safe to talk about your trauma experiences and any symptoms?

7. Review *Telling Your Story.*

8. Introduce this exercise to the group: *Practice telling someone in the room that you are feeling stressed and then say what would be supportive.* Ask the group to break up into dyads, or just ask two of the group members to demonstrate for the whole group to observe and comment.

TELLING YOUR STORY*

 **Handout**

Going through a traumatic experience (military, family, personal history, etc.) can fracture your connection to the world, your family, friends, and yourself. This session is about reconnecting through telling your story. Connecting with others can be part of the healing journey.

A "normal" reaction to trauma is to seal it off from yourself and from others.

Telling your story can be gradual—it does not mean a full disclosure in one conversation. It means opening up about something that has deeply impacted you.

How to talk to your partner (or other SUPPORTIVE adults):

> Choose times when your partner is not distracted or pressed for time. Ask that time be set aside to talk about something important. Consider hiring a babysitter if you have children. Establish a start and a stop time.
> Tell your partner *before* beginning how you would like her to respond. You may find that you would prefer that she not interrupt, or ask questions, or be upset if you begin to get emotional.
> What to talk about: You don't have to tell the whole story, or even start with the hard or most difficult parts.
> Ask for a cool-down time—and talk with your partner about more lighthearted experiences before ending.

Typical mistakes:

> Believing that you can only talk about your experiences with others who have gone through the same thing
> Believing that if you share anything you must share all of it

---

*Adapted from Armstrong, K., Best, S., & Domenici, P. (2005). *Courage after fire: Coping strategies for troops returning from Iraq and Afghanistan and their families*. Berkeley, CA: Ulysses Press. May not be reproduced without permission.

HOMEWORK: PREPARATION FOR TELLING YOUR STORY

 **Handout**

Who might be a supportive adult (your partner, family members, friends) with whom you can share?

1.

2.

3.

How would you like this person to respond?

1.

2.

3.

What parts of your personal experiences are safe to share? Provide information for at least one of the following:

What were the circumstances?

How has the experience affected you and your hopes for the future?

Any symptom from these traumatic experiences that bothers you? How are you healing from your experiences? (Consider sharing coping strategies you are learning.)

What details are important to share first?

Thanks to Karen L. Schoenfeld-Smith, PhD, for these guidelines. May not be reproduced without permission.

Session 23

HURTING THE ONES YOU LOVE

Materials

Emotional Abuse and Mind Games
Relationship Respect Contract

Program

1. Ask each group member to report one "gratitude."

2. Focus on the "mindfulness" exercise for 1 minute.

3. Review the homework from the previous week.

4. Review the *Weekly Check-Ins* and use these to help guide the group discussion in the first half of the group.

5. Review and discuss *Emotional Abuse and Mind Games*.

6. Guide the group members through the following exercise (adapted from Stosny, personal communication, 2001):

   Recall the most hurtful thing you have ever done or said to a loved one. All of us have certainly said or done something hurtful to a parent, child, wife, or girlfriend. Close your eyes for a moment and recall that event. . . . Now imagine strangers doing or saying that same thing to that person. How would you respond?

   The typical response among many group members is *I'd kill them*. Attachment includes an automatic instinct to protect, which is why, without thinking about it, we would jump in front of a bullet to protect our children.

   Then ask: *Isn't it confusing to realize that some of the very mean things you have done—to the people you love the most—are the ones that you would be most outraged by if you observed someone else doing them?*

   Use this basic exercise as a springboard for a discussion about the extremely confusing and conflicted pattern of hurting people whom you love.

   Also, ask the group members to identify the specific scene they visualized and to identify specifically how they might have reacted if they observed someone else acting this way to their partner or kids. This is an excellent opportunity to hear how clearly the group members can identify their own past abusive behavior.

EMOTIONAL ABUSE AND MIND GAMES

 **Handout**

Like physical aggression, repeated emotional abuses can have severe effects on the other person's sense of self and sense of reality. These mind games sometimes leave more lasting damage than physical aggression itself. The person on the receiving end—male or female—may question his or her reality, feel powerless, become overdependent, and so forth. Here are some examples:

Coercion
- *"I am going to kill myself if you leave me!"*
- *"Either you put out for me or I'm going to go find someone who will!"*
- *"I'm gonna take these kids right now and you'll never see them again!"*
- *"I'll get a doctor to say you're crazy and put you away!"*

Put-downs
- *"You're just like your mother: a fat, brainless ass!"*
- *"You're just like your father: a lazy, bull-headed ass!"*
- *"My wife can't cook for shit."* [in front of other people]
- *"My mother was right about you—you'll never amount to anything!"*
- *"How come a big, strong guy like you can't make more money around here?"*
- *"You're stupid."*
- *"You're acting crazy."*
- *"There you go again—crying like a big baby."*
- *"Nobody's ever going to want you!"*

Isolation
- *"I want to know everywhere you've been in the last 24 hours!"*
- *"I want to know where every penny has been spent!"*
- *"I know you go to that school just so you can try to pick up some girl!"*
- *"Your family just messes you up—I don't ever want you to talk to them again!"*
- *"No, you can't have the car. I might need it and you don't need to go anywhere."*
- *"You can't go out. I want you to stay right at home with me."*

Blaming
- *"It's your fault my career is going nowhere."*
- *"Nobody else has ever made me violent! You must be doing something to cause this!"*

Control
- *"You don't even know how to take care of yourself without me around!"*
- *"You have not cleaned up this house properly!"*
- *"I'll decide how the money gets spent!"*
- *"No wife of mine is going out to work—that's my job!"*
- *"I don't care what you think about my gambling habit—it's my money and I'll do what I want!"*
- *"So what if I bought that car without discussing it with you?"*

May not be reproduced without permission.

RELATIONSHIP RESPECT CONTRACT

 **Handout**

We respect each other and our relationship, and we agree that our relationship will only have a chance to be successful if none of the following behaviors take place:

1. No incidents of direct physical abuse or violence.

2. No direct or implied threats of physical abuse or violence (to self, others, or property).

3. No direct or implied threats to behave in a way that would be extremely harmful to the other person (such as exposing personal secrets).

4. No physical restrictions on either party's freedom of movement.

5. No significant property destruction as an expression of aggression.

6. No threats to leave the relationship (except for temporary "Time-Outs" to defuse a tense situation).

7. No pattern of extreme verbal put-downs, character assassinations, or other humiliating acts.

8. No acts of infidelity or behaviors that suggest infidelity.

9. No pattern of lying or deception.

10. No pattern of abusing alcohol or drugs.

Other: _____

_____

Both parties also agree to make all reasonable efforts to focus the therapy sessions on building the positive aspects of the relationship rather than using the session as an opportunity to simply report the bad behavior of the other party.

_____   _____
Name   Date

_____   _____
Name   Date

_____
May not be reproduced without permission.

HOMEWORK

 **Handout**

Review the *Relationship Respect Contract* with your wife or partner. Discuss each item to make sure you both understand and agree. If there is any item that you do not agree on, cross it off. If there are additional ones you both want, add them to the list. Sign the contract. If you are not currently in a relationship, edit the contract in the way that you would like it to be for your next relationship.

May not be reproduced without permission.

Session 24

APOLOGIES

Materials

The Art of Apologies
Classic Apology Mistakes

Program

1. Ask each group member to report one "gratitude."

2. Focus on the "mindfulness" exercise for 1 minute.

3. Review the homework from the previous week.

4. Review the *Weekly Check-Ins* and use these to help guide the group discussion in the first half of the group.

5. Discuss the importance of genuine apologies in close relationships. It is especially important to frame the act of apologizing as something a real man is secure enough and honorable enough to do.

6. Review *The Art of Apologies*. Discuss each item thoroughly and review the possible exceptions to these principles.

7. Review *Classic Apology Mistakes*.

8. Assign homework.

THE ART OF APOLOGIES

 **Handout**

Apologies grease the wheels of most successful relationships. The art of delivering a sincere and well-timed apology is one that all of us should be very skilled at.

The obvious trigger situation for an apology is when you realize that you have done something that has hurt someone you care about. Even if your action was not intended to hurt or you were not aware of how it would affect the other person, an apology is still in order.

An effective apology requires three distinct elements to make it more likely to be well received (which is, after all, the point of the apology in the first place):

1. THE BASIC STATEMENT: "I'm sorry." No rationalizations, no excuses, no hedging. Just a simple statement that you are sorry and what you are sorry for having done. It could be big or very minor; it doesn't matter.

   Start by describing exactly what you did wrong, then just acknowledge that this was a mistake. Accept responsibility:

   I'm really sorry I started teasing you in front of your friends.
   I feel terrible for having that affair and I am really, really sorry for how I have hurt you!
   Sorry I forgot to take out the trash.

2. DEMONSTRATION OF INSIGHT: You need to offer the other person some evidence that you have learned something or that there was some temporary circumstance that will not happen again, or at least that you will really be on guard against it the next time around:

   I think I was just feeling insecure, and this was some sort of way to make jokes and fit in! I won't let that happen again.
   There's no excuse—it had everything to do with me and feeling like I'm not getting enough attention. I wish there was some way I could go back in time and talk to you about what I've been going through instead of doing what I did!
   I was just really rushing around last night and I didn't pay attention. I'm going to start writing it in my appointment book to make sure I remember each week.

3. BEHAVIOR CHANGE: The proof is in the pudding. All the words and all the good intentions in the world don't mean a thing unless the other person sees, over time, that you have genuinely learned something from your mistake and that you are handling a similar situation differently in the future (maybe not 100% perfectly, but definitely better). Remember that your partner cannot possibly feel secure until she has observed, over time, that you have changed. Obviously, the length of time that this takes is directly related to how serious the "crime" was.

May not be reproduced without permission.

CLASSIC APOLOGY MISTAKES

 **Handout**

1. **Not being genuine.** How do you like it when you hear "I'm sorry you feel that way" or "I'm sorry if that hurt your feelings"? Sometimes that might be okay, but most of the time this does not show sincere regret. In fact, it often makes the other person feel stupid for "overreacting" or being "too sensitive." This usually does not get a passing grade as a genuine apology.

2. **Crummy body language.** Maybe the words are right, but there is no eye contact or even a hostile look. Or the tone of voice sounds sarcastic. This also fails the grade.

3. **Waiting for the perfect moment.** Some people wait for the "perfect moment" for an apology, but this does not exist (although it's probably best not to do in heavy traffic or when the baby is screaming). The perfect moment to apologize is the moment you realize you've done something wrong or as soon as possible thereafter.

4. **Expecting immediate and total forgiveness.** Remember Commandment #5: We do not have control over any other person, but we do have control over ourselves. All you can do is give it your best and most sincere shot. She may never be able to forgive you, or it may take her a little while.

5. **Apologizing too much.** Some people apologize way too much, for the smallest things, or even when they haven't really done anything wrong. This is just plain irritating, and it's like crying wolf. The real and significant apologies will be weakened if they distract attention from real issues. This weakens meaningful apologies when the time for them arrives.

May not be reproduced without permission.

HOMEWORK

 **Handout**

Identify three apologies to offer to your wife or partner or children. Make the apology, and record the response from the other person. If you are not in contact with any of them, identify three apologies you would make if you had the opportunity.

1. Apology from you:

Response from wife, partner, or child:

2. Apology from you:

Response from wife, partner, or child:

3. Apology from you:

Response from wife, partner, or child:

May not be reproduced without permission.

Session 25

WHAT'S UP WITH SEX?

Materials

> *Sexual Abuse: Psychological and Physical*
> *Masculinity Traps: Sex*
> *Sexual Meaning Questionnaire*

Program

1. Ask each group member to report one "gratitude."

2. Focus on the "mindfulness" exercise for 1 minute.

3. Review the homework from the previous week.

4. Review the *Weekly Check-Ins* and use these to help guide the group discussion in the first half of the group.

5. This session is particularly complicated for group discussion. Many of the group members, who may have become less defensive about general actions of psychological and physical abuse, may continue to maintain considerable defensiveness about examples of what we are describing as sexual abuse.

   Some of this is simply from ignorance or lack of awareness about why certain behaviors qualify as abusive. First of all, it is important to simply define sexual abuse: any unwanted touching or other sexual behavior is a form of abuse. If it involves intercourse, it is rape. If it involves physical force, it is sexual assault. It doesn't matter if the assaulter is drunk, stoned, or feeling pressured by his friends—it is still rape or sexual assault. And it doesn't matter if the two parties know each other, have had sex before, or even if they are married. It is still considered rape or sexual assault.

6. With these definitions in mind, review the *Sexual Abuse: Psychological and Physical* handout. Discuss the various ways in which sexual behaviors can represent an abuse of power in the relationship. Obviously, not all of the examples on the list are criminal offenses, but they represent a continuum of sexually abusive behaviors.

7. As you guide this discussion, be especially sensitive to the embarrassment or discomfort that the group members are likely to experience. Some may joke around

or join in laughter about degrading comments toward women. Although it is important to set a different tone in this group, be careful about confronting too intensely—unless all else fails. Power struggles will doom this group discussion. Set an example by maintaining a serious tone yourself. Calmly remind the men of the importance of talking about these issues in ways that do not degrade or generalize. If they are able to describe examples of some of these destructive sexual behaviors in others, this may be an acceptable way to generate valuable discussion and reflection.

8. Review *Masculinity Traps: Sex* and the *Sexual Meaning Questionnaire*. It is especially important to focus on issues of entitlement and perceived peer pressure in this discussion. Refer back to Session 9 on jealousy and misinterpretations; remind the men, through examples, how crucial their self-talk is when they encounter some form of sexual frustration.

SEXUAL ABUSE: PSYCHOLOGICAL AND PHYSICAL

 **Handout**

Sexual abuse is one of the rooms in the *House of Abuse* that is especially difficult to talk about. Sometimes it is even difficult to know that it is taking place. Below is a sample of different forms of abusive sexual behaviors, both psychological and physical. If you can, try to be honest with yourself about which of these you may have used at some point in your relationships.

Put-Downs:

> Making jokes about women in your wife's or partner's presence
> Checking out other women in her presence
> Making sexual put-down jokes
> Comparing her body to those of other women or to pictures in magazines
> Criticizing sexual performance
> Blaming her if you don't feel satisfied with sex
> Using sexual labels: calling her a "slut" or "frigid"

Mind Games:

> Telling her that agreeing to sex is the only way she can prove she has been faithful or that she still loves you
> Revealing intimate details about her to others
> Withholding sex and affection only to gain control over her
> Engaging in sexual affairs

Pressure:

> Always wanting sex
> Expecting sex whenever you want it
> Demanding sex with threats
> Talking her into stripping or talking sexually in a way that feels humiliating to her
> Talking her into watching sex or pornography when this is offensive to her
> Talking her into touching others when this is offensive to her

Force:

> Forcing touch
> Forcing sex while she's sleeping
> Touching her in ways that are uncomfortable to her
> Forcing uncomfortable sex
> Forcing sex after physical abuse
> Sex for the purpose of hurting (use of objects/weapons)

May not be reproduced without permission.

MASCULINITY TRAPS: SEX

 **Handout**

Masculinity traps	The big picture
I deserve to have sex upon demand.	*Sex involves the needs of two people, not just one.*
If my wife or partner doesn't put out, it means she's trying to hurt me.	*There are many reasons why she may not be in the mood for sex.*
Real men get laid all the time.	*Many men talk big—real men respect the individuality of the woman they love.*
I've had a hard day. I deserve some rewards.	*I can't expect her to always be available exactly when I need her.*

May not be reproduced without permission.

SEXUAL MEANING QUESTIONNAIRE

 **Handout**

Rate the importance of the various functions of sex in your life by circling the number that best describes how you feel about each item.

Function of sex in your life	Not important				Very important		
1. Produce children	1	2	3	4	5	6	7
2. Orgasm for me	1	2	3	4	5	6	7
3. Orgasm for my partner	1	2	3	4	5	6	7
4. Reassurance of my masculinity	1	2	3	4	5	6	7
5. Reassure my partner of her femininity	1	2	3	4	5	6	7
6. Expression of love/warmth by me	1	2	3	4	5	6	7
7. Expression of love/warmth by her	1	2	3	4	5	6	7
8. Way to release tension	1	2	3	4	5	6	7
9. Way to prove my sexual skills	1	2	3	4	5	6	7
10. Part of relationship responsibility	1	2	3	4	5	6	7
11. Way to have fun	1	2	3	4	5	6	7
12. Way to make up after argument or conflict	1	2	3	4	5	6	7
13. Way of exercising power and control	1	2	3	4	5	6	7
14. Way of curing boredom	1	2	3	4	5	6	7
15. Way to reduce stress	1	2	3	4	5	6	7

May not be reproduced without permission.

HOMEWORK

   **Handout**

Based on your own life experience, prepare three messages or words of advice you would want to pass on to your son (or what you would suggest a father should pass on to his son) about how to handle sex in a meaningful relationship.

1.

2.

3.

May not be reproduced without permission.

Session 26

KIDS WHO WITNESS

Materials

The Great Santini *video* (the kitchen fighting scene begins at 1:28:29 and ends at 1:29:57)
When Kids See Their Parents Fight
Kids' Exposure to Destructive Conflicts
Questions for Kids

Program

1. Ask each group member to report one "gratitude."

2. Focus on the "mindfulness" exercise for 1 minute.

3. Review the homework from the previous week.

4. Review the *Weekly Check-Ins* and use these to help guide the group discussion in the first half of the group.

5. Discuss the effects on kids of witnessing domestic violence. Begin by explaining that abusive fighting—verbal and physical—affects not only the adults, but also the children who witness it. Emphasize that children usually have excellent radar for tuning in to this behavior, even if the parents are sure it is all happening behind closed doors.

6. Play *The Great Santini* (the kitchen fighting scene begins at 1:28:29 and ends at 1:29:57) and discuss. Review the ways in which each child has his or her own specific reaction to the violence. Identify self-talk for the children and the parents.

7. Review *When Kids See Their Parents Fight* and *Kids' Exposure to Destructive Conflicts*. Ask the group members to identify any of these symptoms they have noticed in their own kids. Also ask them to recall experiences when they were growing up and witnessed violence between their parents.

8. Review *Questions for Kids*. **This is the most important component of this session.** Select several group members who have children who have witnessed abusive behavior in this family to role-play. The group member should answer the questions, asked in detail by the group leaders and group members. Review the self-talk and emotions. It is often helpful to have the "kids" talk to each other about what it has been like for them.

WHEN KIDS SEE THEIR PARENTS FIGHT

 Handout

They will often display symptoms like these, without always being able to tell you what is bothering them:

SLEEP PROBLEMS: fears of going to sleep, nightmares, dreams of danger

MYSTERIOUS ACHES AND PAINS: headaches, stomachaches, medical problems like asthma, arthritis, ulcers

FEARS: anxiety about being hurt or killed, fears of going to school or of separating from the mother, worrying, difficulties concentrating and paying attention

BEHAVIOR PROBLEMS: abusing drugs or alcohol, suicide attempts or engaging in dangerous behavior, eating problems, bedwetting or regression to earlier developmental stages, acting perfect, overachieving, behaving like small adults

PEOPLE PROBLEMS: losing interest in people, fighting or abusing others, outbursts of temper, tantrums

EMOTIONAL PROBLEMS: losing interest in activities, feeling lonely

May not be reproduced without permission.

KIDS' EXPOSURE TO DESTRUCTIVE CONFLICTS

 **Handout**

Kids usually know what is happening when their parents are fighting. Studies indicate that kids are very aware of the level of domestic violence in the house. In a recent study, 80% to 90% of kids reported that they witnessed (heard or saw) their parents fighting, even when a vast majority of the parents insisted that the kids didn't know what was going on.

Exposure to fighting makes kids more sensitive. Although it is commonly believed that kids who are exposed to parents' fighting "get used to it," studies actually indicate that they become more sensitive with exposure. As we might expect from those who have posttraumatic stress disorder, kids from violent homes become more upset when they are exposed to adults in conflict, rather than less.

Certain factors seem to make kids' reactions worse.
>   Conflict-related factors: The more intense and nasty the conflict, the more severe the kids' symptoms are likely to be.
>   Topic: *"Are they arguing about me?"* If the child perceives that the argument is about him or her, the symptoms are usually worse.
>   Resolution: Are the adults able to resolve the conflict? If that child observes that the adults are able to calm down and maturely recover, his or her symptoms are usually reduced. There is a little less chaos and a little less to be frightened of.
>   Child involvement: The more actively involved the child is in trying to intervene or break up the conflict, the more severe the symptoms.
>   Child's age: The younger the child, the more likelihood there is for self-blame and for believing *"This must be about me!"*
>   Gender: Boys are more likely to blame themselves.

Future relationship behavior is affected. Boys who observe domestic violence are six times more likely to commit similar acts as an adult; girls who witness are much more likely to become abusive themselves or to find partners who are abusive.

The good news is that not all kids are so negatively affected by witnessing adults in destructive conflicts. A good relationship between the child and adult and greater capacity to talk honestly about feelings about what has happened serve as a buffer to some of these effects. Thus, for reasons that we cannot quite explain, some kids are simply constitutionally more adaptable to bad situations.

May not be reproduced without permission.

QUESTIONS FOR KIDS*

 Handout

In this exercise, group members take turns role-playing, being the child in their house who has witnessed violence. Other group members interview these "kids" about their experiences.

1. What kinds of things do your mom and dad fight about?

2. What happens when your mom or dad gets angry or your parents fight? Can you describe any fights between your parents that you saw yourself? What did you see or hear during the fight? What was it like for you afterward (e.g., did you see your parents' injuries or the house torn apart)? What were your reactions?

3. What do you do if your parents push, shove, or hit each other? Do you leave the room or go outside?

4. Can you describe any fights between your parents in which you were caught in the middle, or when you tried to stop them? What happened?

5. Do they ever fight about you? How does this make you feel (scared, confused, sad, mad)?

6. Do you talk to anybody about this?

7. How do you handle your feelings since this has happened? Do you ever feel like hurting yourself or anyone else?

8. In an emergency for you or your parents, who would you call? Where could you go?

---

*Adapted with permission from the Family Violence Prevention Fund's publication entitled *Domestic Violence: A National Curriculum for Family Preservation Practitioners*, written by Susan Schecter, MSW, and Anne L. Ganley, PhD. May not be reproduced without permission.

HOMEWORK: KID STORIES*

 **Handout**

Complete the following exercise and bring it for group review next session.

1. **You are an 8-year-old boy**, and you really like playing video games more than anything else. Your dad has been getting drunk lately. He comes home and hits your mom, and he breaks things after he thinks the kids have gone to sleep. Your older sister has started using drugs and running away. One day after school, your mom says you're all going to be moving away from your dad, with her, to another town across the state, near your aunt and uncle. Your mom tells you that she can't trust your dad anymore and that you kids might be the next to get hurt. You've never seen your dad hit your sister, and he's never hit you.

   How would you feel when you heard about your mom's plans?

   How would you feel toward her?

   How would you feel toward your father?

2. **You are a 10-year-old girl** who's been really screwing up at school lately. Your dad is constantly on your case; it seems like nothing you do is right. You know your mom has been spending a lot of money, and he is always yelling at her about it. One time he locked her out of the house, and she had to stay outside in the rain until you snuck around the back to let her in. She yells right back at him, calling him bad names. Sometimes she even throws things at him and you can hear things breaking. You and your mom have left a couple of times for a few days, but she always comes back. It's hard for you to sleep. You want this to stop, and you ask if you can live with somebody else for a while.

   How would you feel toward your mother?

   How would you feel toward your father?

---

*Adapted with permission from the Family Violence Prevention Fund's publication entitled *Domestic Violence: A National Curriculum for Family Preservation Practitioners*, written by Susan Schecter, MSW, and Anne L. Ganley, PhD. May not be reproduced without permission.

PART VI

THE RELATIONSHIP ABUSE/SUBSTANCE ABUSE LEVEL II SUPPLEMENT

SUBSTANCE ABUSE/ DOMESTIC VIOLENCE PROGRAMMING

Treatment programs throughout the country are developing interventions that target specific types of domestic violence offenders.

This is especially relevant when there is a clear correlation between substance abuse and incidents of domestic violence. In these cases, programs have been developed that place special emphasis on the role of alcohol and other drugs in the lives of these men.

San Diego County, for example, has instituted a pilot program known as the Level System. Level I groups are for domestic violence offenders without any obvious substance abuse problems.

Level II groups are for offenders with some clear correlation between substances and domestic violence. These offenders attend the standard group format with special emphasis on the role of substance abuse.

Level III offenders have a more serious addiction to substances, and they attend a concurrent outpatient substance abuse treatment program.

Level IV offenders are the most serious substance abusers, requiring inpatient treatment programs for substance abuse, with the domestic violence programs following after this treatment is completed.

SUPPLEMENTARY PROGRAMMING FOR LEVEL II SUBSTANCE ABUSE/DOMESTIC VIOLENCE GROUPS

The guidelines below are designed to supplement the core content of the STOP Program with a strong, consistent emphasis on substance abuse issues and their relationship to errors in judgment, behavioral impulsivity, and aggression in relationships.

When conducting a Level II group, integrate these questions and discussion points into the standard core curriculum of each session.

Session 1: THE RED FLAGS OF ANGER

1. When discussing the red flags of anger, make sure to identify any drinking or using as one kind of red flag.
2. Apply the concept of "red flags of anger" to "red flags of using."
3. Explore alternatives to using.

Session 2: ANGER STYLES

1. Discuss how alcohol and other substances are likely to make each of the anger styles more severe.
2. Discuss how much more frequently people engage in emotional abuse when they are in an altered state, because substances affect both perception and judgment.

Session 3: TRAUMA AND ANGER

1. Identify ways in which the group members may have used substances to cope with effects of trauma.

Session 4: MINDFULNESS AND GRATITUDES

1. Discuss how mindfulness can be used to avoid drinking or using.
2. Discuss how gratitudes can be used to avoid drinking or using.

Session 5: SELF-TALK AND PERSONAL STORIES

1. Apply the "bad rap" concept to rationalizations for using:

    I've had a bad day—I deserve to have a drink!

2. Discuss how "bad rap" cognitions can make someone more likely to use.

Session 6: THE BROKEN MIRROR

1. Discuss how the "broken mirror" experience can lead someone to use (escapism).
2. With the *Affliction* video, discuss the possible role that alcohol is playing in the man's unhappiness and defensiveness.

Session 7: MASCULINITY TRAPS AND TOUGH GUISE

1. Identify the ways in which many men might say that "Men are supposed to . . . be able to drink, use, and party." Discuss what happens to men who choose to not do much drinking or using.

Session 8: MASCULINITY TRAPS: GUIDELINES FOR GOOD MEN

1. Discuss the pressures on "real men" to drink and use.
2. Discuss the effects of the father's drinking on his behavior in the scene from *The Great Santini*.

Session 9: JEALOUSY AND MISINTERPRETATIONS

1. Discuss how jealousy can often be triggered by cognitive distortions that are exaggerated by alcohol or drugs.
2. Discuss the ways in which judgment and decision making are impaired when someone is under the influence, so that they might overreact (sometimes violently) when they feel threatened.

Session 10: MISATTRIBUTIONS AND NEGATIVE INTERPRETATIONS

1. Ask the group members to identify ways in which they put more negative spin on situations when they are under the influence. Go through each of the four categories (Attribution of Hostility, External, Hostile Reaction, and Overgeneralization).

Session 11: SUBSTANCE ABUSE AND RELATIONSHIP ABUSE: WHAT'S THE CONNECTION?

No extra content needed.

Session 12: ACCOUNTABILITY

1. When discussing accountability defenses, make sure to emphasize *I was drunk; what can I say?*
2. In the *Accountability Statement*, discuss the ways in which intoxication has been used as a way to rationalize aggressive behavior.

Session 13: PUT-DOWNS FROM PARENTS

1. Ask the group members to identify how much of their parents' put-downs were related to drugs or alcohol.
2. Ask the group members to identify times when their own use of alcohol or drugs has led them to behave more aggressively with their own kids.

Session 14: SHAME-O-PHOBIA

1. Ask the group members what an alcoholic or drug user is most likely to do right after the kind of fight they witnessed in *Good Will Hunting.*
2. Discuss how chemical dependency is often based on shame and guilt. In some cases the addict started to use in order to offset feelings of shame and guilt, and in almost every case the addict now lives with shame and guilt based on things he did to others.

Session 15: SURVIVOR GUILT AND MORAL INJURY

1. Identify the ways that people use substances to cope with negative feelings associated with guilt, shame, and failure.

Session 16: SWITCH!

1. Compare the "old self-talk" that takes place while under the influence of alcohol or drugs to the "new self-talk" that is likely to be more clear-thinking.
2. Identify ways in which group members have been more effective in managing their destructive behaviors when they are clean and sober.
3. The content of the "Switch!" session may focus on the decision to use in addition to the decision to be aggressive or violent.

Session 17: ASSERTIVENESS AND ASKING FOR CHANGE

1. Discuss how the use of substances and addiction affects communication styles, leading to extremes of passivity/withdrawal or aggression.
2. Discuss the effects of substance abuse on communication patterns, involving secrets, dishonesty, and blaming.
3. Discuss how trying to ask for behavioral change from other people is less likely to succeed if they mistrust the person because of a history of alcohol or drug use.
4. Ask the group members to monitor how much their "Keeping Track" homework situation tempted them to drink or use.

Session 18: HANDLING CRITICISM

1. Discuss how drugs and alcohol can interfere with the ability to handle criticism.
2. Ask the group members to monitor how much their "Keeping Track" homework situation tempted them to drink or use.

Session 19: FEELINGS, EMPATHY, AND ACTIVE LISTENING

1. Discuss how intoxication and patterns of abuse can interfere with the abilities to hear what another person is saying or to offer "active listening" responses.

2. Ask the group members to monitor how much their "Keeping Track" homework situation tempted them to drink or use.

Session 20: INTIMACY TRAINING: WIVES AND PARTNERS GROUP

1. Discuss how intoxication and patterns of abuse can interfere with the ability to understand where the other person is coming from.
2. In the homework assignment, instruct the group members to include substance abuse patterns in their essay.

Session 21: FOUR HORSEMEN OF THE APOCALYPSE

1. Discuss how substance abuse can increase the presence of the *Four Horsemen of the Apocalypse*.
2. Identify ways in which intoxication and patterns of abuse can interfere with the ability to manage conflicts effectively and to stay respectful of one's partner.

Session 22: INTIMACY TRAINING: TELLING YOUR TRAUMA STORY TO YOUR PARTNER

1. Identify ways that meaningful conversations can take a wrong turn when *either* person is under the influence of alcohol or drugs.
2. Ask for examples when it has actually been easier to "tell your story" when slightly under the influence of alcohol or drugs.

Session 23: HURTING THE ONES YOU LOVE

1. Discuss the ways in which the incidents recalled in the visualization exercise were influenced by drugs or alcohol.
2. Discuss additions to the *Relationship Respect Contract* regarding drinking and using.

Session 24: APOLOGIES

1. Discuss the importance of making amends based on destructive behaviors resulting from substance abuse.

Session 25: WHAT'S UP WITH SEX?

1. Discuss the impact of drugs and alcohol on sex, including increased or decreased drive, increased selfish sexual behavior, lapses in judgment, and so on.

Session 26: KIDS WHO WITNESS

1. Identify the role of alcohol in the violent scene from *The Great Santini*.
2. Discuss the following regarding the exposure of kids to substance abuse:
   a. Children are typically aware if a parent is abusing drugs and/or alcohol.
   b. Even young children are aware that certain substances that their parents ingest are "special" and will alter their parents' behavior in ways that most other things will not.

    c. While parents are engaging in substance abuse, children are often the victims of abuse and neglect.

    d. While parents are engaging in substance abuse, children are often forced to grow up too fast and take on adult responsibilities in order to make up for unavailable parents.

    e. Children are influenced by the rules that often exist in addicted families, such as "keeping secrets." These are often unspoken rules that may lead to shame and guilt.

NEW MEMBER SESSION I: HOUSE OF ABUSE

1. Add a room for substance abuse to the *House of Abuse*.

NEW MEMBER SESSION II: TIME-OUT

1. Review how much more difficult it is to effectively implement a Time-Out if one or both partners have been drinking or using.
2. Emphasize the extreme importance of not drinking or using during a Time-Out.

EXIT/RELAPSE PREVENTION SESSION I: MOST VIOLENT AND/OR MOST DISTURBING INCIDENT

1. Help the group members focus on the role that substances played in this incident.

EXIT/RELAPSE PREVENTION SESSION II: PREVENTION PLAN

1. Identify the ways in which the *Prevention Plan* may be especially valuable for situations in which the person has been drinking or using.

PART VII
STANDARD FORMS

GUT CHECK QUESTIONNAIRE*

 **Handout**

Name _____ Date _____

Answer each of these questions as honestly as you can. None of these answers will be shared with the group without your consent. Use a number from 1 to 10, with 1 being lowest and 10 being highest. When answering questions 4, 5, and 6, remember that the purpose of this is simply to offer some valuable feedback to one of your peers. Most of us have trouble seeing ourselves without honest feedback from others who care about us.

1. How honest am I being in the group?   *(Not at all/Completely)* _____ (1–10)

2. How much effort am I putting into the group?   *(None/Very Much)* _____ (1–10)

3. How much feedback am I giving to others in the group? *(None/Very Much)* _____ (1–10)

4. Whom do I know the most/least in the group?

    Most   _____

    Least   _____

5. Who is acknowledging responsibility for his relationship problems most in the group?

    Most   _____

6. Who is being the most emotionally honest in the group?

    Most   _____

7. How much am I getting out of the group?

1	2	3	4	5	6	7	8	9	10
Nothing		A little			Some		A lot	Very Much	

*Adapted from Dutton (1995). May not be reproduced without permission.

WEEKLY CHECK-IN

 **Handout**

Name _____ **Date** _____

1. **SUCCESS.** Describe one way in the past week in which you successfully kept yourself from being aggressive or successfully used something you learned in group. The success can be large or small. This is a chance to "pat yourself on the back."
   What was the situation?

   What might you have done in the past?

   What did you do right?

Calmly stood up for my rights		Told myself to relax		Took a Time-Out	
Expressed my feelings responsibly		Changed my self-talk		Other	

2. **SUBSTANCE USE.** Please remember that the first question the court, probation officer, or other referring agency will ask, when they receive knowledge that you have used, is "Was the treatment provider aware of this?" If we were aware of it, we can tell them, "Yes, and here is what we're doing to help him or her." Over the course of the last week did you use any of the following?

Alcohol (only report if you are prohibited from drinking as part of your probation mandate)	
Methamphetamine	
Cocaine	

If you answered "yes" to any of the above, please describe the circumstances, and the thought you

used that gave you permission._____

_____

_____

May not be reproduced without permission.

3. **PROBLEM SITUATION.** Describe one way in the past week in which you did not handle an interpersonal situation well.

   What was the situation?

   How upset did you feel?

   | 1 | 10 | 20 | 30 | 40 | 50 | 60 | 70 | 80 | 90 | 100 |

   Not At All Upset   Upset   Extremely Upset

   How did you respond?

4. **AGGRESSION.** Did you become verbally or physically aggressive toward anyone in the past week (including threats and damage to property)?

Slapping		Kicking		Grabbing/ restraining	
Punching/ hitting		Property destruction		Throwing things	
Verbal/ emotional abuse		Sexual abuse		Other	

   What would you do in a similar situation in the future to avoid becoming aggressive?

5. **HOMEWORK.** Did you complete homework for the week?

   Yes _____

   No _____

   None Assigned_____

EVALUATION FORM

Handout

This form is to be completed at the end of the group member's 13th, 26th, 39th, and 52nd sessions (for a 52-week program), as well as at any other time when there are special recommendations or concerns.

Group Member's Name: _____

Group Leaders' Names: _____

_____

Group Attended: _____ Dates: _____ to _____

Total # sessions attended: _____ Date of report: _____

Please evaluate the group member on all the scales listed below. The norm group should be the overall population of group members at this stage of treatment. Give a "1" for the lowest score on each item and a "9" for the highest score, with any number in between that best describes your assessment.

PARTICIPATION

No personal self-disclosure	1 2 3 4 5 6 7 8 9	Appropriate self-disclosure
Defensive	1 2 3 4 5 6 7 8 9	Very open to feedback
Feedback aggressive/destructive	1 2 3 4 5 6 7 8 9	Feedback constructive
Does not complete homework	1 2 3 4 5 6 7 8 9	Completes homework

BEHAVIOR

Poor ability expressing feelings	1 2 3 4 5 6 7 8 9	Excellent ability
Does not recognize responsibility for family violence	1 2 3 4 5 6 7 8 9	Recognizes responsibility
Poor control over impulses and behavior	1 2 3 4 5 6 7 8 9	Good control
Minimal empathy/concern for victim or other family members	1 2 3 4 5 6 7 8 9	Excellent empathy/concern
Little self-awareness of buildup of tension or emotional needs	1 2 3 4 5 6 7 8 9	Excellent self-awareness
Poor assertive expression of needs and feelings	1 2 3 4 5 6 7 8 9	Excellent assertiveness

Please rate the group member's overall progress, **as compared to the overall population of group members at this stage of treatment**. Rate on a scale of 1 to 9, with 1 as no improvement and 9 as outstanding improvement.

1   2   3   4   5   6   7   8   9   N/A

_____

May not be reproduced without permission.

At this time, check the box if you recommend either of the following:

Probation_____

Termination from program_____

COMMENTS

_____

_____

_____

_____

_____

_____

_____

Group leader signature _____

Group leader signature _____

TREATMENT EXPECTATIONS*

 **Handout**

Here are some basic guidelines about what treatment programs typically expect from group members at various stages of their treatment. These expectations are based on a 52-week program and may be adapted depending on the length of treatment.

Treatment Expectations for Weeks 1–12

1. PARTICIPATION: Arrives on time, attentive, asks questions, constructive contribution to group discussions, is able to describe incident that brought him or her to program

2. ATTITUDE: Uses respectful language, demonstrates gender respect, respect for group process and other members, accountability for actions

3. HOMEWORK: Completed as assigned, shows thought and effort

4. BASIC SKILLS: Uses "I statements," reports appropriate use of Time-Outs, identifies "red flags," uses listening skills

Treatment Expectations for Weeks 13–25

1. PARTICIPATION: Arrives on time, attentive, asks questions, constructive contribution to group discussions, willingness to voluntarily participate

2. ATTITUDE: Uses respectful language, demonstrates gender respect, respect for group process and other members, accountability for actions

3. HOMEWORK: Completed as assigned, shows thought and effort

4. BASIC SKILLS: Uses "I statements," reports appropriate use of Time-Outs, identifies "red flags," uses listening skills

5. ADVANCED SKILLS: Reflective listening, utilizes compromise and negotiation tools, identifies personal strengths and weaknesses (positive change and areas of concern), uses noncontrolling communication

Treatment Expectations for Weeks 26–39

1. PARTICIPATION: Arrives on time, attentive, asks questions, constructive contribution to group discussions, willingness to voluntarily participate, initiates constructive dialogue, appropriately challenges others

2. ATTITUDE: Uses respectful language, demonstrates gender respect, respect for group process and other members, accountability for actions, consistent modeling of positive changes in behavior and attitude

---

*Adapted from San Diego County Domestic Violence Standards (County of San Diego Probation Department, 2012). May not be reproduced without permission.

3. HOMEWORK: Completed as assigned, shows better developed thought and effort

4. BASIC SKILLS: Consistent use of "I statements," reports appropriate use of Time-Outs, identifies "red flags," uses listening skills

5. ADVANCED SKILLS: Consistent use and modeling of skills: reflective listening, utilizing compromise and negotiation tools, identifying personal strengths and weaknesses (positive change and areas of concern), using noncontrolling communication, reports use of new skills in current relationships

Treatment Expectations for Weeks 40–52

1. PARTICIPATION: Arrives on time, consistently attentive, asks questions, constructive contribution to group discussions, willingness to voluntarily participate, initiates constructive dialogue, appropriately challenges others

2. ATTITUDE: Uses respectful language, demonstrates gender respect, respect for group process and other members, accountability for actions, consistent modeling of positive changes in behavior and attitude, maintains self-confidence and commitment to nonviolence

3. HOMEWORK: Completed as assigned, shows better developed thought and effort, approved relapse prevention plan accomplished

4. BASIC SKILLS: Maintains consistent use of "I statements," reports appropriate use of Time-Outs, identifies "red flags," uses listening skills

5. ADVANCED SKILLS: Consistent use and modeling of skills: reflective listening, utilizing compromise and negotiation tools, identifying personal strengths and weaknesses (positive change and areas of concern), using noncontrolling communication; positive modeling for other group members; demonstrates empathy for victim, children, and others

REFERENCES

Amherst H. Wilder Foundation. (1995). *Foundations for violence-free living: A step-by-step guide to facilitating men's domestic abuse groups*. St. Paul, MN: Author.

Armstrong, K., Best, S., & Domenici, P. (2005). *Courage after fire: Coping strategies for troops returning from Iraq and Afghanistan and their families*. Berkeley, CA: Ulysses Press.

Bankart, P. (2006). *Freeing the angry mind*. Oakland, CA: New Harbinger Publications.

Basch, M. F. (1988). *Understanding psychotherapy: The science behind the art*. New York, NY: Basic Books.

Carr, R. B. (2011). Combat and human existence: Toward an intersubjective approach to combat-related PTSD. *Psychoanalytic Psychology, 28*(4), 471–496.

County of San Diego Probation Department. (2012). San Diego County Domestic Violence Treatment Standards (personal communication, February 15, 2013).

Dutton, D., & Golant, S. (1995). *The batterer: A psychological profile*. New York, NY: Basic Books.

Dutton, D. G. (1998). *The abusive personality: Violence and control in intimate relationships*. New York: Guilford Press.

Dutton, D., van Ginkel, C., & Strazomski, A. (1995). The role of shame and guilt in the intergenerational transmission of abusiveness. *Violence and Victims, 10*(2), 121–131.

Engel, L. B., & Ferguson, T. (1990). *Imaginary crimes: Why we punish ourselves and how to stop*. New York, NY: Houghton Mifflin.

Englar-Carlson, M., & Stevens, M. A. (2006). *In the room with men: A casebook of therapeutic change*. Washington, DC: American Psychological Association.

Erickson, M., & Rossi, E. (1979). *Hypnotherapy: An exploratory casebook*. New York, NY: Irvington.

Geffner, R., & Mantooth, C. (1995). *A psychoeducational model for ending wife/partner abuse: A program manual for treating individuals and couples*. Tyler, TX: Family Violence and Sexual Assault Institute.

Gilligan, S. (1987). *Therapeutic trances*. New York, NY: Brunner Mazel.

Good, G. (1995). Male gender role conflict, depression, and help seeking: Do college men face double jeopardy? *Journal of Counseling and Development, 74*(1), 70.

Gottman, J. (2000). *The seven principles for making marriage work*. New York, NY: Three Rivers Press.

Henretty, J. R., & Levitt, H. M. (2010). The role of therapist self-disclosure in psychotherapy: A qualitative review. *Clinical Psychology Review, 30*(1), 63–77.

Holtzworth-Munroe, A., & Hutchinson, G. (1993). Attributing negative intent to wife behavior: The attributions of maritally violent versus nonviolent men. *Journal of Abnormal Psychology, 102*(2), 206–211.

Holtzworth-Munroe, A., Meehan, J., Herron, K., Rehman, U., & Stuart, G. (2000). Testing the Holtzworth-Munroe and Stuart (1994) Batterer Typology. *Journal of Consulting and Clinical Psychology, 68*(6), 1000–1019.

Holtzworth-Munroe, A., & Stuart, G. (1994). Typologies of male batterers: Three subtypes and the differences among them. *Psychological Bulletin, 116*, 476–497.

Hornby, N. (1995). *High fidelity*. New York: Riverhead Books.

Johnson, M. P., & Ferraro, K. J. (2000). Research on domestic violence in the 1990s: Making distinctions. *Journal of Marriage & the Family, 62*(4), 948–963.

Johnson, M. P. (2008). *A typology of domestic violence: Intimate terrorism, violent resistance, and situational couple violence* (Northeastern Series on Gender, Crime, and Law). Holliston MA: Northeastern.

Lambert, M., & Barley, D. (2002). Research summary on the therapeutic relationship and psychotherapy outcome. In J. C. Norcross (Ed.), *Psychotherapy relationships that work: Therapist contributions and responsiveness to patients* (pp. 17–32). New York: Oxford University Press.

Levant, R., & Pollack, W. (1995). *A new psychology of men.* New York, NY: Basic Books.

Millon, T., Millon, C., Davis, R., & Grossman, S. (2006). *Millon Clinical Multiaxial Inventory—III.* Minneapolis, MN: Pearson Assessments.

O'Hanlon, W., & Weiner-Davis, M. (1989). *In search of solutions.* New York, NY: W. W. Norton.

O'Neil, J. (2008). Summarizing 25 years of research on men's gender role conflict using the Gender Role Conflict scale: New research paradigms and clinical implications. *The Counseling Psychologist, 36*(3), 358–445.

Pence, E., & Paymar, M. (1993). *Education groups for men who batter: The Duluth model.* New York, NY: Springer.

Pollack, W., & Levant, R. (1998). *New psychotherapy for men.* New York, NY: John Wiley & Sons.

Potter-Efron, R., & Potter-Efron, P. (1995). *Letting go of anger: The eleven most common anger styles and what to do about them.* Oakland, CA: New Harbinger.

Rabinowitz, F. E. (2006). Crossing the no cry zone: Doing psychotherapy with men. Retrieved from http://www.continuingedcourses.net/active/courses/course026.php

Real, T. (1997). *I don't want to talk about it: Overcoming the secret legacy of male depression.* New York, NY: Scribner.

Resick, P. A., Monson, C. M., & Chard, K. M. (2007). *Cognitive processing therapy: Veteran/Military version.* Washington, DC: Department of Veterans Affairs.

Schechter, S., & Ganley, L. (1995). *Domestic violence: A national curriculum for family preservation practitioners.* San Francisco, CA: Family Violence Prevention Fund.

Shapiro, S. (1995). *Talking with patients: A self psychological view of creative intuition and analytic discipline.* Lanham, MD: Jason Aronson.

Walker, L. (1980). *The battered woman.* New York: Harper & Row.

Weiss, J., & Sampson, H. (1986). *The psychoanalytic process: Theory, clinical observations, and empirical research.* New York, NY: Guilford Press.

Welland, C., & Ribner, N. (2010). Culturally specific treatment for partner-abusive Latino men: A qualitative study to identify and implement program components. *Violence and Victims, 25*(6), 799–813.

Wexler, D. B. (1991). *The adolescent self: Strategies for self-management, self-soothing, and self-esteem in adolescence.* New York, NY: W. W. Norton.

Wexler, D. B. (2004). *When good men behave badly: Change your behavior, change your relationship.* Oakland, CA: New Harbinger.

Wexler, D. B. (2006). *Is he depressed or what: What to do when the man you love is irritable, moody, and withdrawn.* Oakland, CA: New Harbinger.

Wexler, D. B. (2009). *Men in therapy: New approaches for effective treatment.* New York, NY: W. W. Norton.

Wexler, D. B. (2010). Shame-o-phobia. *Psychotherapy Networker, 34*(3), 20–51.

Wexler, D. B. (2013). Approaching the unapproachable—Therapist self-disclosure to de-shame male clients. In A. Rochlen & F. Rabinowitz (Eds.), *Breaking barriers in counseling men: Insights and innovations.* New York: Routledge.

Yalom, I. (1995). *The theory and practice of group psychotherapy* (3rd ed.). New York, NY: Basic Books.

INDEX

In this index, page numbers in **bold** denote handouts and page numbers in *italics* denote homework.